An Introduction to Modern English Grammar

HAYDEN ENGLISH LANGUAGE SERIES

Consulting Editor—Robert W. Boynton

Principal of the Senior High School
Germantown Friends School

An Introduction to Modern English Grammar

JEAN MALMSTROM

Professor of English, Western Michigan University

HAYDEN BOOK COMPANY, INC., NEW YORK

The author would like to thank the proprietors for permission to quote copyrighted works, as follows:

SHERWOOD ANDERSON: from "I'm a Fool." Reprinted by permission of Harold Ober Associates Incorporated. Copyright © 1924 by Eleanor Anderson, copyright renewed.

RICHARD ARMOUR: from *It All Started with Columbus.* Copyright 1953, © 1961 by Richard Armour. Published by McGraw-Hill Book Company. Used by permission.

ENID BAGNOLD: from *National Velvet.* Published by Wm. Morrow & Company, Inc. Copyright 1935 by Enid Bagnold Jones. Permission for distribution in the United States granted by Brandt & Brandt.

SAUL BELLOW: from *Seize the Day.* Copyright © 1956 by Saul Bellow. Reprinted by permission of The Viking Press, Inc.

RAY BRADBURY: from "The Crowd" and "The Man Upstairs." From *The October Country,* copyright 1955 by Ray Bradbury. Reprinted by permission of The Harold Matson Company, Inc.

BENNETT CERF: from *The Laugh's On Me.* Copyright © 1959 by Bennett Cerf. Reprinted by permission of Doubleday & Company, Inc.

WALTER VAN TILBURG CLARK: from *The Ox-bow Incident.* Reprinted with permission of the publisher. Copyright 1954. Published by Random House, Inc.

WILLIAM J. COUGHLIN: from "The Great Mokusatsu Mistake." Copyright © 1954, by Harper's Magazine, Inc. Reprinted from the March 1954 issue of *Harper's Magazine* by permission of the author.

E. E. CUMMINGS: "spring is like a perhaps hand." Copyright, 1925, by E. E. Cummings. Reprinted from his volume *Poems 1923-1954* by permission of Harcourt, Brace & World, Inc. "La Guerre: the bigness of cannon." Copyright 1923, 1951, by E. E. Cummings. Reprinted from his volume *Poems 1923-1954* by permission of Harcourt, Brace & World, Inc.

ROBERT FROST: "A Prayer of Spring" and "Two Tramps in Mud Time." From *Complete Poems of Robert Frost,* copyright 1934 by Holt, Rinehart and Winston, Inc. Copyright 1936, (c) 1962 by Robert Frost. Copyright (c) 1964 by Lesley Frost Ballantine. Reprinted by permission of Holt, Rinehart and Winston, Inc.

ERNEST HEMINGWAY. Excerpts from various works of Ernest Hemingway that appear in this book are protected by copyright and have been reprinted here by special permission of Charles Scribner's Sons.

LOUIS HJELMSLEV: from *Prolegomena to a Theory of Language.* Reprinted with permission of the copyright owners, the Regents of the University of

---

Second printing, April 1968

 Library of Congress Catalog Card Number 67-30055. Printed in the United States of America.

Wisconsin, from Louis Hjelmslev, *Prolegomena to a Theory of Language,* Francis J. Whitfield, translator, 1961, The University of Wisconsin Press.

GERARD MANLEY HOPKINS: from "Spring" and "Spring and Fall: to a young child." Reprinted from *Poems of Gerard Manley Hopkins* by permission of Oxford University Press, Inc. Copyright 1948.

PAULINE HYLKEMA: from "Discovery." *Calliope,* Winter, 1959, Western Michigan University.

BEL KAUFMAN: from *Up the Down Staircase.* © 1964 by Bel Kaufman. Published by Prentice-Hall, Inc., Englewood Cliffs, New Jersey.

CLYDE KLUCKHOHN: from *Mirror for Man.* Copyright 1949 by McGraw-Hill Book Company. Published by McGraw-Hill Book Company. Used by permission.

JOHN KNOWLES: from *A Separate Peace.* Reprinted with permission of the publisher. Copyright 1959, John Knowles.

FELICIA LAMPORT: "Hint," "Cretion," "Astrous Ending," and "Fine Old Professor." From *Scrap Irony.* Reprinted by permission of the publisher, Houghton Mifflin Company.

D. H. LAWRENCE: from "The Rockinghorse Winner." From *Complete Short Studies* by D. H. Lawrence. Copyright 1933 by the Estate of D. H. Lawrence, © 1961 by Anthony Ravagli & C. Montague Weekley, Executors of the Estate of Frieda Lawrence Ravagli. Reprinted by permission of the Viking Press, Inc.

HARPER LEE: from *To Kill a Mockingbird.* Copyright (c) 1960 by Harper Lee. Published by J. B. Lippincott Company.

ARCHIBALD MACLEISH: "You Andrew Marvell." From *The Collected Poems of Archibald MacLeish.* Reprinted by permission of the publisher, Houghton Mifflin Company.

DAVID MCCORD: "Gloss." From *Odds Without Ends,* by permission of Little, Brown and Co. Copyright 1953 by David McCord.

JOHN MCCRAE: "In Flanders Fields." Reprinted from *In Flanders Fields and Other Poems* by permission of Putnam's Coward-McCann. Copyright.

H. L. MENCKEN: from *The American Language.* Abridged by Raven I. McDavid, Jr. Alfred A. Knopf, Inc. Copyright 1963.

JAMES A. MICHENER: from *The Bridge at Andau.* Reprinted with permission of the publisher. Copyright 1957 by Random House, Inc. Published by Random House, Inc. From *The Bridges at Toko-Ri.* Reprinted with permission of the publisher. Copyright 1953 by Random House, Inc. Published by Random House, Inc.

A. A. MILNE: "Politeness." From *When We Were Very Young.* Copyright, 1924, by E. P. Dutton & Co., Inc. Renewal, 1952, by A. A. Milne. Reprinted by permission of the publishers.

OGDEN NASH: "A Strange Casement of the Poetic Apothecary." From *Everyone But Thee And Me.* By permission of Little, Brown and Co. Copyright (c) 1962 by Ogden Nash.

STERLING NORTH: from *So Dear to My Heart.* Copyright 1947 by Sterling North. Reprinted by permission of the author and Doubleday & Company, Inc.

FLANNERY O'CONNOR: from "A Circle in the Fire." From *A Good Man Is Hard to Find,* published by Harcourt, Brace & World, Inc. Reprinted by permission of the publisher.

WILFRED OWEN: "Anthem for Doomed Youth." From *The Collected Poems of Wilfred Owen.* Copyright © by Chatto and Windus, Ltd., 1963. Reprinted by permission of the publisher, New Directions Publishing Corporation, Chatto and

To Jean, Michele, and Margaret,
my granddaughters,

in the sincere hope that they will have a better time of it in English class than their mothers did

---

Preface

In this book, *grammar* means "the machinery of language." As native speakers of English we know English grammar because we have been using it for years to communicate with other speakers of English. However, knowing how to use English grammar does not necessarily mean understanding it. This book employs modern methods of analysis to help you understand your knowledge of English grammar. Because great writers possess exceptional skill in handling the machinery of language, throughout this book literature demonstrates and exemplifies grammar in action.

After a brief foreword explaining the advantages of understanding modern English grammar, Chapter One, "Language and Situation," discusses five interacting dimensions of appropriate grammatical usage. Every time we use English, we (1) either speak or write (2) more or less formally (3) in a specific place (4) at a definite time in our life and in the history of the world, and (5) we reveal our education or lack of it. Appropriate language matches its situation on all five dimensions. Literature comments abundantly on this fact. For example, Mark Twain writes about three New England poets confusing a California miner by talking writing. At a mad tea-party, Lewis Carroll's Alice in Wonderland is disgusted by the mixed-up language of the Mad Hatter, the March Hare, and the Dormouse. Sherwood Anderson parallels the language of the high school dropout with his failure in love.

Chapter Two, "Learning the Grammar of English," shows children learning their native language—listening to their elders, imitating what they hear, playing with words, using analogy, and grasping the deep grammar of their language by sudden flashes of insight. By the time they are ready for school, they have mastered parts of speech and sentence patterns. A galaxy of writers illuminates these amazing achievements: Ruth Hirsch

Weir, Kornei Chukovsky, Jean Berko, Leo S. Vygotsky, Hugh Walpole, Walter Van Tilburg Clark, Robert Ruark, John Knowles, James A. Michener, Mary Roberts Rinehart, D. H. Lawrence, Joseph Conrad, and Stephen Crane, among others.

Chapter Three, "Transformation of Sentences," explains that children learn much more than parts of speech and simple sentence patterns. They also learn how to ask questions, to join sentences together, and to reduce sentences to fragments and insert them into other sentences. These more complicated sentences are the results of transformations. The work of any writer can reveal his use of transformations. Among those chosen in this chapter are Saul Bellow, Flannery O'Connor, Herman Wouk, Joseph Conrad, Ray Bradbury, Edwin Arlington Robinson, Siegfried Sassoon, and John Steinbeck.

Chapter Four, "Sentences and Non-sentences," proves that we can tell the two apart. A non-sentence is an ungrammatical word-group that only a foreigner would produce. We do not distort our grammar as foreigners do. A fable by James Thurber undergirds this discussion. On the other hand, poets often stretch grammar for poetic effect, but never so far as to create a non-sentence. To observe poets' ways with English grammar, we examine poems by Robert Browning, Robert Frost, E. E. Cummings, and Gerard Manley Hopkins, among others.

Chapter Five, "The Horizons of Grammar: Ambiguity," reveals that language is naturally ambiguous because (1) words have more than one meaning, (2) words shift their part of speech, and (3) transformations hide structure. However, when we add context, we often remove ambiguity. That literature clarifies these points is massively demonstrated by quotations from Sir Walter Scott, Christopher Marlowe, Thomas Hardy, Shakespeare, Michael Drayton, Richard Armour, Dr. Samuel Johnson, Thomas Hood, James Joyce, Bennett Cerf, and Leo Rosten.

Chapter Six, "The Horizons of Grammar: Variety," focuses first on variety in words. Ogden Nash, Mark Twain, and Joseph Conrad comment on the importance of the exactly right word, and Hemingway brings the northern Michigan woods to life by using the exactly right words. Then James Stephens and William Blake each revise a poem, making their words more precise and varied. Secondly, this chapter considers variety in sentences. Starting from John Erskine's statement that we sharpen sentences by adding details, we see how professional writers keep a central sentence intact within their larger sentences and add to it at both ends. We analyze and imitate sentences by such writers as Katherine Anne Porter, F. Scott Fitzgerald, Elizabeth Bowen, Willa Cather, Elizabeth Parsons, William Faulkner, James Baldwin, Eudora Welty, Robert Penn Warren, and John Updike.

This description of English grammar is not complete, because completeness is not a sensible goal for a book about grammar. Man's knowledge of his language far exceeds the largest grammar book that can ever be written. This book surfaces just enough of our subconscious knowledge of English grammar to give us tools and self-confidence for analyzing literature and our own writing more intelligently than we could otherwise.

Acknowledgments

The original manuscript of *An Introduction to Modern English Grammar* could not have been written without the professional collaboration of Mrs. Dean Margaret Hauck, Consultant on High School English Teaching, and Richard Boyd Hauck, her husband, Assistant Professor of English, University of Washington. I am deeply grateful to them.

I owe later debts to the many English teachers who, as students at Western Michigan University, studied the book in manuscript and made suggestions for its improvement. I especially thank the thirty-nine participants in our NDEA Institute during the summer of 1966. In this connection, two of my colleagues deserve thanks. Professor Ralph N. Miller, as director of the Institute, made the manuscript available to the participants. I thank him for his generosity. Professor Robert A. Palmatier, my fellow-teacher in the Institute, used the manuscript in his applied linguistics class, as I did in mine. I appreciate his cooperation and favorable comments.

Finally I am beholden to four other persons. My editors, Peter R. Stillman, Robert W. Boynton, and S. William Cook, Jr., gave creative criticism and expert help. My husband, Vincent F. Malmstrom, completely disregarding his own convenience, was adviser and expediter in a thousand ways during the composition of this book.

Table of Contents

Foreword: Reasons for Studying Language

Language is the key to all human activities and institutions. Through it we understand our world; without it we are isolated and helpless. Helen Keller, sightless and deaf, was unable to learn language in the nearly effortless way we acquired it. Until her parents arranged for a brilliant, determined tutor, Helen's childhood world was a place of dark and silent ignorance. The revelation of language came to her suddenly and miraculously:

> We walked down the path to the well-house, attracted by the fragrance of the honeysuckle with which it was covered. Some one was drawing water and my teacher placed my hand under the spout. As the cool stream gushed over one hand she spelled into the other the word water, first slowly, then rapidly. I stood still, my whole attention fixed upon the motions of her fingers. Suddenly I felt a misty consciousness as of something forgotten a thrill of returning thought, and somehow the mystery of language was revealed to me. I knew then that "w-a-t-e-r" meant the wonderful cool something that was flowing over my hand. That living word awakened my soul, gave it light, hope, joy, set it free! There were barriers still, it is true, but barriers that could in time be swept away.
>
> From *The Story of My Life*
> by Helen Keller.

THE NATURE AND IMPORTANCE OF LANGUAGE

A language is a set of symbols by which humans communicate. These symbols can be either spoken or written, but in every civilization and in every person, the vocal symbol-system precedes the written symbol-system. People speak before they write, both as individuals and as nations. In fact, most languages today have no writing system.

Before we enter first grade we have learned to speak and understand our language. Every normal child performs this miracle with his native language in the first five or six years of his life. Thereby he establishes his membership in the human community, for no other living organism uses language.

This amazing human invention, language, has moved sober scholars to wonder. Here is a famous Danish linguist, Louis Hjelmslev, writing about language.

> Language—human speech—is an inexhaustible abundance of manifold treasures. Language is inseparable from man and follows him in all his works. Language is the instrument with which man forms thought and feeling, mood, aspiration, will and act, the instrument by whose means he influences and is influenced, the ultimate and deepest foundation of human society. But it is also the ultimate, indispensable sustainer of the human individual, his refuge in hours of loneliness, when the mind wrestles with existence and the conflict is resolved in the monologue of the poet and the thinker.
>
> From *Prolegomena to a Theory of Language*
> translated by Francis J. Whitfield.

Possessing language from an early age, why should we then study it? There are practical reasons, which we will discuss in turn. But far more important, we should learn deeply about language because it is man's towering achievement. How it works, its structures, the ways in which it influences thought and behavior—these are the concerns of anyone who would know more about man and his ideas.

PRACTICAL USES OF LANGUAGE STUDY

An immediately practical reason for learning about language is to develop a technical vocabulary for discussing the grammatical problems of writing, reading, speaking, and listening. Grammar is the machinery that makes language work, and anyone who uses language is using grammar to produce the consistent patterns of his language. But while we all have a grammar machine built into our heads, we may lack a clear understanding of how it operates and may be unable to utilize it fully in solving complex communication problems.

If we understand the technical words *pronoun* and *predicate,* for instance, we can efficiently discuss the problem of whether to use the pronoun *I* or *me* in the predicate after *is.* We can quickly understand when the teacher explains the basic problems clustering around the use of pronouns in United States speech today, and we can weigh the possible courses of action open to us in the pronoun area. We can decide to avoid the problem by using some form other than *It's I* or *It's me;* we can decide to disregard the problem by saying *It's me;* we can decide to follow the instructions of our teacher in the classroom but talk as we please outside the classroom. The point is that with a formal knowledge of language we can clearly understand the problem and react to it analytically instead of with ignorance.

What other practical reasons can we find? What occupations can you think of that require at least some technical knowledge of grammar?

Consider the areas of computer technology and communications engineering. On October 4, 1957, Sputnik I flashed into the sky, alerting the United States to Russia's advanced technology and our apparent need to catch up to her. United States scientists and engineers could not study the books and articles the Russians had written on rocketry and space; but the Soviets could read our scientific and technical writing because they had studied English in their schools and universities.

One quick way to solve the language problem was suggested: program an electronic computer to take in Russian and print out an English translation. This meant, however, that first we would have to analyze both grammars for similarities and differences and then program the computer to handle all these factors. The U.S. Army, Navy, and Air Force, the National Science Foundation, and several large foundations have appropriated huge sums of money for the project; but thus far it has met with only moderate success.

Computers will probably never produce translations that can stand alone without editing by human translators. In the early 1950's, when machine translation was just beginning, some professional translators feared that computers would put them out of work. Quite the contrary has happened; translators have become more valuable and their work has grown more interesting. Now the computer performs the mechanical drudgery of producing a rough version of the translation. Human translators then apply their creative skills to perfecting the computer's garbled output. The result is a larger quantity of translation of a higher quality.

The translator at the United Nations has special need for grammatical knowledge. Most of the translation is simultaneous. That is, the translator listens and translates just one word-group behind the actual speaker. The translator must know the grammar of two languages so thoroughly that he can actually "think in two languages." These translators are paid very well, simply because this ability is rare and therefore valuable. Grammar is of its essence.

Anthropologists need a knowledge of grammar too. Indeed, many of the great developments in modern language study in the United States have resulted directly from a union of anthropology and modern grammar. When anthropologists wanted to study the Indian civilizations of our great Southwest, they could not make any real progress until they had unlocked the secrets of their languages. Teams of anthropologists and linguists—modern English grammarians—worked together. As Clyde Kluckhohn, the anthropologist, writes in *Mirror for Man:*

> Perhaps the most important contribution of anthropological linguistics has come from the difficulties the anthropologist goes through in trying to express the meanings contained in speech structures completely foreign to the pattern of all European tongues. This study and this experience have forced upon the anthropologist a rather startling discovery which is fraught with meaning for a world where peoples speaking many different idioms are trying to communicate without distortions. Every language is something more than a vehicle for exchanging ideas and information—more even than a tool for self-expression and for letting off emotional steam or for getting other people to do what we want.
>
> Every language is also a special way of looking at the world and interpreting experience. Concealed in the structure of each different language are a whole set of unconscious assumptions about the world and life in it. The anthropological linguist has come to realize that the general ideas one has about what happens in the world outside oneself are not altogether "given" by external events. Rather, up to a point, one sees and hears what the grammatical system of one's language has made one sensitive to, has trained one to look for in experience. This bias is the more insidious because everyone is so unconscious of his native language as a system. To one brought up to speak a certain language it is part

> of the very nature of things, remaining always in the class of background phenomena. It is as natural that experience should be organized and interpreted in these language-defined classes as it is that the seasons change. In fact the naïve view is that anyone who thinks in any other way is unnatural or stupid, or even vicious—and most certainly illogical.

In order to understand the anthropologist's grammatical difficulties as Clyde Kluckhohn explains them, we can study how the Hopi language looks at the world and interprets experience.[1] Hopi is a "timeless" language. That is, whereas English always must include a time signal in its sentences, Hopi has no grammatical machinery for doing so. To us events happen in past, present, or future time. Hopi ignores time but includes grammatical signals denoting various relationships among the speaker, the hearer, and the total situation. Hopi speakers use the same verb form, *wari,* to express present time, "he is running," and past time, "he ran." However, to the Hopi, the difference between observed running and remembered running—both past in time—demands separate verb forms: *wari* and *era wari.* We say "he ran" in both cases. English and Hopi do not agree in their "unconscious assumptions about the world and life in it," as Kluckhohn says. We speak English and therefore we think in English. The Hopi language structures the universe differently for the Hopi thinkers.

The speech therapist working with brain-damaged patients reports that the grammatical parts of a language are lost in a definite order: first, function words, then adjectives, adverbs, verbs, and nouns, in that order. As the patient recovers he gains back the parts of his grammar in the same sequence but in reverse order: nouns, verbs, adverbs, adjectives, and function words. Analysis and treatment of speech disorders would be quite difficult for the therapist without a solid background in grammar.[2]

Of course, the English teacher and the foreign language teacher need a knowledge of English grammar in order to do their jobs. All that we have already said presupposes that these

---

[1] See "Science and Linguistics" in *Language, Thought, and Reality, Selected Writings of Benjamin Lee Whorf,* John B. Carroll, ed. (New York: The Technology Press of M.I.T. and John Wiley and Sons, Inc., 1956), p. 213.

[2] See *Selected Conference Papers of the National Association of Foreign Student Affairs,* English Language Section, 1962, p. 49.

teachers are thoroughly grounded in the grammatical machinery of their native tongue, to be able to explain it to the students and to know which points are important and in what ways.

Writers too need a firm grasp of grammar. The more the poet or novelist understands the language code, the better he can mold it to his purposes and exploit its beauty. The poet John Woods says:

> A poem is a participation in language, and language is capable of confusing the best intentions of both reader and writer. I think of language as a living thing, a connective tissue between individuals, between institutions, between past and present: its verbs are muscles . . .; its nouns are germ plasm; its syntax is its shapeliness (or its ugliness).
>
> The idea, then, does not leap fully articulated from one mind to another. It must risk its self in the guts of language. To say is to change.[3]

No man is an island. He is linked to his fellow men by language.

Below is a fascinating—and quite grim—story concerning a tragic misuse of language. After you have read it, write a brief paper on the importance of understanding the ways of language in today's complex world. (You might also again refer to Clyde Kluckhohn's statement.)

The Great *Mokusatsu* Mistake

> When Premier Suzuki confronted the press on July 28, he said that the cabinet was holding to a policy of *mokusatsu*. The word *mokusatsu* not only has no exact counterpart in English but it is ambiguous even in Japanese. Suzuki, as we know, meant that the cabinet had decided to make no comment on the Potsdam proclamation, with the implication that something significant was impending. But the Japanese were tricked by their own language. For in addition to meaning "to withhold comment," *mokusatsu* may also be translated as "to ignore."
>
> The word has two characters in Japanese. *Moku* means "silence" and *satsu* means "kill," thus implying in an absolutely literal sense "to kill with silence." This can mean—to a Japanese—either to ignore or to refrain from comment.

[3] From "The Arrival of the Racers" in *Readings for Communication* (Third edition), Anne Oas Szalkowski, ed. (Western Michigan University, 1961), p. 388.

(The word Suzuki should have used was *mokushi.* The character *shi* means "to observe" and in Japanese the phrase "to observe silence" can be taken only one way. Then there could have been no possibility whatsoever of a mistranslation of the word.)

Unfortunately the translators at the Domei News Agency could not know what Suzuki had in mind. As they hastily translated the prime minister's statement into English, they chose the wrong meaning. From the towers of Radio Tokyo the news crackled to the Allied world that the Suzuki cabinet had decided to "ignore" the Potsdam ultimatum.

The cabinet was furious at Suzuki's choice of words and the subsequent error by Domei. The reaction of Kase, who had fought long and hard for peace, was one of dismay.

"This was a piece of foolhardiness," he says. "When I heard of this I strongly remonstrated with the cabinet chief secretary, but it was too late. . . . Tokyo radio flashed it—to America! The punishment came swiftly. An atomic bomb was dropped on Hiroshima on August 6 by the Allies, who were led by Suzuki's outrageous statement into the belief that our government had refused to accept the Potsdam proclamation."

But for this tragic mistake, Kase laments, Japan might have been spared the atomic attack and the Russian declaration of war.

An Introduction to Modern English Grammar

CHAPTER ONE

Language and Situation

INTRODUCTION

When we were very young, we were often told, "*Please* and *thank you* are magic words." Even then, we were learning word manners, just as we learned table manners. We even learned that certain words were "bad" and should not be used.

Here is a poem about a little boy who has been taught polite word manners. He has learned the proper response to the adults' question, "How are you?" even though he sometimes wishes they would not ask it.

Politeness

If people ask me,
I always tell them:
"Quite well, thank you, I'm very glad to say."
If people ask me,
I always answer, 5
"Quite well, thank you, how are you today?"
I always answer,
I always tell them,
If they ask me
Politely 10
BUT SOMETIMES
I wish
That they wouldn't.

From *When We Were Very Young*
by A. A. Milne.

In the following story of a mixed-up tea-party, Alice tries to be polite, but she thinks that the Mad Hatter, the March Hare, and the Dormouse are all trying to be difficult. Although the conversation is in English, it has no clear meaning for her. Alice is completely confused, but her confusion only adds to our fun in watching them use English in maddening ways. They ask her a riddle that has no answer; they talk about time as if it were a person; they change "Twinkle, Twinkle, Little Star" to "Twinkle, Twinkle, Little Bat." Alice finally walks away in disgust.

A Mad Tea-Party

There was a table set out under a tree in front of the house, and the March Hare and the Hatter were having tea at it: a Dormouse was sitting between them, fast asleep, and the other two were using it as a cushion, resting their elbows on it, and talking over its head. "Very uncomfortable for the Dormouse," thought Alice; "only as it's asleep, I suppose it doesn't mind."

The table was a large one, but the three were all crowded together at one corner of it. "No room! No room!" they cried out when they saw Alice coming. "There's *plenty* of room!" said Alice indignantly, and she sat down in a large arm-chair at one end of the table.

"Have some wine," the March Hare said in an encouraging tone.

Alice looked all round the table, but there was nothing on it but tea. "I don't see any wine," she remarked.

"There isn't any," said the March Hare.

"Then it wasn't very civil of you to offer it," said Alice angrily.

"It wasn't very civil of you to sit down without being invited," said the March Hare.

"I didn't know it was *your* table," said Alice: "it's laid for a great many more than three."

"Your hair wants cutting," said the Hatter. He had been looking at Alice for some time with great curiosity, and this was his first speech.

"You should learn not to make personal remarks," Alice said with some severity: "it's very rude."

The Hatter opened his eyes very wide on hearing this; but all he *said* was, "Why is a raven like a writing-desk?"

"Come, we shall have some fun now!" thought Alice. "I'm glad they've begun asking riddles—I believe I can guess that," she added aloud.

"Do you mean that you think you can find out the answer to it?" said the March Hare.

"Exactly so," said Alice.

"Then you should say what you mean," the March Hare went on.

"I do," Alice hastily replied; "at least—at least I mean what I say—that's the same thing, you know."

"Not the same thing a bit!" said the Hatter. "Why, you might just as well say that 'I see what I eat' is the same thing as 'I eat what I see'!"

"You might just as well say," added the March Hare, "that 'I like what I get' is the same thing as 'I get what I like'!"

"You might just as well say," added the Dormouse, which seemed to be talking in its sleep, "that 'I breathe when I sleep' is the same thing as 'I sleep when I breathe'!"

"It *is* the same thing with you," said the Hatter, and here the conversation dropped, and the party sat silent for a minute, while Alice thought over all she could remember about ravens and writing-desks, which wasn't much.

The Hatter was the first to break the silence. "What day of the month is it?" he said, turning to Alice: he had taken his watch out of his pocket, and was looking at it uneasily, shaking it every now and then, and holding it to his ear.

Alice considered a little, and then said, "The fourth."

"Two days wrong!" sighed the Hatter. "I told you butter wouldn't suit the works!" he added, looking angrily at the March Hare.

"It was the *best* butter," the March Hare meekly replied.

"Yes, but some crumbs must have got in as well," the Hatter grumbled: "you shouldn't have put it in with the breadknife."

The March Hare took the watch and looked at it gloomily: then he dipped it into his cup of tea, and looked at it again: but he could think of nothing better to say than his first remark, "It was the *best* butter, you know."

Alice had been looking over his shoulder with some curiosity. "What a funny watch!" she remarked. "It tells the day of the month, and doesn't tell what o'clock it is!"

"Why should it?" muttered the Hatter. "Does *your* watch tell you what year it is?"

"Of course not," Alice replied very readily: "but that's because it stays the same year for such a long time together."

"Which is just the case with *mine,*" said the Hatter.

Alice felt dreadfully puzzled. The Hatter's remark seemed to her to have no sort of meaning in it, and yet it was certainly English. "I don't quite understand you," she said, as politely as she could.

"The Dormouse is asleep again," said the Hatter, and he poured a little hot tea upon its nose.

The Dormouse shook its head impatiently, and said, without opening its eyes, "Of course, of course: just what I was going to remark myself."

"Have you guessed the riddle yet?" the Hatter said, turning to Alice again.

"No, I give it up," Alice replied. "What's the answer?"

"I haven't the slightest idea," said the Hatter.

"Nor I," said the March Hare.

Alice sighed wearily. "I think you might do something better with the time," she said, "than wasting it in asking riddles that have no answers."

"If you knew Time as well as I do," said the Hatter, "you wouldn't talk about wasting *it.* It's *him.*"

"I don't know what you mean," said Alice.

"Of course you don't!" said the Hatter, tossing his head contemptuously. "I dare say you never even spoke to Time!"

"Perhaps not," Alice cautiously replied; "but I know I have to beat time when I learn music."

"Ah! That accounts for it," said the Hatter. "He won't stand beating. Now, if you only kept on good terms with him, he'd do almost anything you liked with the clock. For instance, suppose it were nine o'clock in the morning, just time to begin lessons: you'd only have to whisper a hint to Time, and around goes the clock in a twinkling! Half-past one, time for dinner!"

("I only wish it was," the March Hare said to itself in a whisper.)

"That would be grand, certainly," said Alice thoughtfully; "but then—I shouldn't be hungry for it, you know."

"Not at first, perhaps," said the Hatter: "but you could keep it to half-past one as long as you liked."

"Is that the way *you* manage?" Alice asked.

The Hatter shook his head mournfully. "Not I!" he replied. "We quarreled last March—just before *he* went mad, you know—" (pointing with his teaspoon at the March Hare) "—it was at the great concert given by the Queen of Hearts, and I had to sing

> *'Twinkle, twinkle, little bat!*
> *How I wonder what you're at!'*

You know the song, perhaps?"

"I've heard something like it," said Alice.

"It goes on, you know," the Hatter continued, "in this way:—

> *'Up above the world you fly,*
> *Like a tea-tray in the sky.*
> *Twinkle, twinkle—'* "

Here the Dormouse shook itself, and began singing in its sleep "*Twinkle, twinkle, twinkle, twinkle—*" and went on so long that they had to pinch it to make it stop.

"Well, I'd hardly finished the first verse," said the Hatter, "when the Queen bawled out 'He's murdering the time! Off with his head!' "

"How dreadfully savage!" exclaimed Alice.

"And ever since that," the Hatter went on in a mournful tone, "he won't do a thing I ask! It's always six o'clock now."

A bright idea came into Alice's head. "Is that the reason so many tea-things are put out here?" she asked.

"Yes, that's it," said the Hatter with a sigh: "it's always

tea-time, and we've no time to wash the things between whiles."

"Then you keep moving round, I suppose?" said Alice.

"Exactly so," said the Hatter: "as the things get used up."

"But what happens when you come to the beginning again?" Alice ventured to ask.

"Suppose we change the subject," the March Hare interrupted, yawning. "I'm getting tired of this. I vote the young lady tells us a story."

"I'm afraid I don't know one," said Alice, rather alarmed at the proposal.

"Then the Dormouse shall!" they both cried. "Wake up, Dormouse!" And they pinched it on both sides at once.

The Dormouse slowly opened its eyes. "I wasn't asleep," it said in a hoarse, feeble voice, "I heard every word you fellows were saying."

"Tell us a story!" said the March Hare.

"Yes, please do!" pleaded Alice.

"And be quick about it," added the Hatter, "or you'll be asleep again before it's done."

"Once upon a time there were three little sisters," the Dormouse began in a great hurry; "and their names were Elsie, Lacie, and Tillie; and they lived at the bottom of a well—"

"What did they live on?" said Alice, who always took a great interest in questions of eating and drinking.

"They lived on treacle,"[1] said the Dormouse, after thinking a minute or two.

'They couldn't have done that, you know," Alice gently remarked. "They'd have been ill."

"So they were," said the Dormouse; "*very* ill."

Alice tried a little to fancy to herself what such an extraordinary way of living would be like, but it puzzled her too much: so she went on: "But why did they live at the bottom of a well?"

"Take some more tea," the March Hare said to Alice, very earnestly.

"I've had nothing yet," Alice replied in an offended tone; "so I can't take more."

"You mean you can't take *less*," said the Hatter: "it's very easy to take *more* than nothing."

"Nobody asked *your* opinion," said Alice.

---

[1] *Treacle:* This is an English name for our molasses. Alice is an English girl and uses English rather than United States names for things. Other examples are *tea-tray* for our tray and *milk-jug* for our milk pitcher.

"Who's making personal remarks now?" the Hatter asked triumphantly.

Alice did not quite know what to say to this: so she helped herself to some tea and bread-and-butter, and then turned to the Dormouse, and repeated her question. "Why did they live at the bottom of a well?"

The Dormouse again took a minute or two to think about it, and then said, "It was a treacle-well."

"There's no such thing!" Alice was beginning very angrily, but the Hatter and the March Hare went "Sh! Sh!" and the Dormouse sulkily remarked, "If you can't be civil, you'd better finish the story for yourself."

"No, please go on!" Alice said very humbly. "I won't interrupt you again. I dare say there may be *one*."

"One, indeed!" said the Dormouse indignantly. However, he consented to go on. "And so these three little sisters—they were learning to draw, you know—"

"What did they draw?" said Alice, quite forgetting her promise.

"Treacle," said the Dormouse, without considering at all this time.

"I want a clean cup," interrupted the Hatter: "let's all move one place on."

He moved on as he spoke, and the Dormouse followed him: the March Hare moved into the Dormouse's place, and Alice rather unwillingly took the place of the March Hare. The Hatter was the only one who got any advantage from the change; and Alice was a good deal worse off than before as the March Hare had just upset the milk-jug into his plate.

Alice did not wish to offend the Dormouse again, so she began very cautiously: "But I don't understand. Where did they draw the treacle from?"

"You can draw water out of a water-well," said the Hatter; "so I should think you could draw treacle out of a treacle-well—eh, stupid?"

"But they were *in* the well," Alice said to the Dormouse, not choosing to notice this last remark.

"Of course they were," said the Dormouse: "well in."

This answer so confused poor Alice, that she let the Dormouse go on for some time without interrupting it.

"They were learning to draw," the Dormouse went on, yawning and rubbing its eyes, for it was getting very sleepy; "and they drew all manner of things—everything that begins with an M—"

"Why with an M?" said Alice.

"Why not?" said the March Hare.

Alice was silent.

The Dormouse had closed its eyes by this time, and was going off into a doze; but, on being pinched by the Hatter, it woke up again with a little shriek, and went on: "—that begins with an M, such as mouse-traps, and the moon, and memory, and muchness—you know you say things are 'much of a muchness'—did you ever see such a thing as a drawing of a muchness?"

"Really, now you ask me," said Alice, very much confused, "I don't think—"

"Then you shouldn't talk," said the Hatter.

This piece of rudeness was more than Alice could bear: she got up in great disgust, and walked off: the Dormouse fell asleep instantly, and neither of the others took the least notice of her going, though she looked back once or twice, half hoping that they would call after her: the last time she saw them, they were trying to put the Dormouse into the teapot.

"At any rate I'll never go *there* again!" said Alice, as she picked her way through the wood. "It's the stupidest tea-party I ever was at in all my life!"

From *Alice in Wonderland*
by Lewis Carroll.

The real reason that Alice is confused at the tea-party is that the language of the Mad Hatter, the March Hare, and the

Dormouse does not fit the situation. Riddles are supposed to be answered; *it* not *he* refers to time; nursery rhymes about stars are not about bats. The language of this tea-party is madly inappropriate, and we laugh at poor Alice's predicament. Lewis Carroll's delightful story points out that inappropriate language can cause our laughter and Alice's disgust. Since normally we do not want to communicate nonsense, how can we choose language appropriate to the situation in which we use it? The answer to this question has five dimensions. That is, we must examine the question from five points of view. These are:

I. Young–Old
II. Spoken–Written
III. Standard–Nonstandard
IV. Formal–Informal–Technical
V. Northern–Midland–Southern

We will discuss each in turn.

DIMENSIONS OF AMERICAN ENGLISH

I. Young–Old

When we communicate with someone much older or much younger than we are, we often have problems. Not only words but also viewpoints and standards differ across generations. Too often speakers miss the importance of this fact, behaving as though the other generation is either stupid or stubborn in failing to understand. The truth is that age is a powerful factor in American English. *Time is an important dimension.*

In *Flower Drum Song*, a musical comedy by Rodgers and Hammerstein, the older and the younger generations have trouble understanding each other. They ask, "How will we ever communicate without communication?" Communication between them is being blocked because the older generation cannot understand the younger generation's slang, and, even more importantly, neither generation can understand the other's attitudes. The older generation feels that the younger has no respect for what its elders say, and the younger wishes it could take over the training of the older. In a song, the younger generation complains:*

> When we are using words the modern way,
> They're much too big
> To try to dig
> The colorful things we say.
> If we could take over the training of the Other Generation,
> We know we could improve them quite a lot.

And a father resents the way his twenty-one year old son talks to him:

> He tells me I am "cukey"
> And "strictly for the birds!"

And both generations moan:

> What are we going to do about the Other Generation?
> How will we ever communicate without communication?

The same problem faces Linus, in this *Peanuts* cartoon, as he tries to communicate with his grandmother.

The little girl in the following poem is too young to know how to punctuate and capitalize, but she understands the young old communication dilemma that exists between her mother and herself.

> my mother said today we are going downtown
> to buy
> a coat for you
> and i said can i pick it out all by my
> self 5
> and she said yes
> i guess
> you can and i said i want it to be
> pink
> and she said well let's think 10
> about it and i knew
> it would be
> navy blue

From *The Split-Level Child*
by Rosalind Welcher.

II. Spoken–Written

Some words are very unlikely in speech; others are very unlikely in writing. Have you ever known anyone who "talked like a book"? This kind of person typically says, "I do not" rather than "I don't," "there is" instead of "there's," and "he cannot" in place of "he can't." Relentlessly he plods through his sentences from capital letter to period, refusing to be interrupted. Because he does not understand that spoken English is different from written English, his speech is likely to be boring and painful to the listener.

On the other hand, authors write spoken English whenever they show people talking. They use dialogue to reveal much about their characters. A skillful writer may use misspellings to suggest that a character is not well educated or that he comes from a certain part of the country. For instance, the author may spell *can't* "kaint" or *both* "bofe." If the author spells *women* "wimmin" or *was* "wuz," he is using *eye dialect.* That is, these misspellings actually reflect the way these words are pronounced by everybody, educated and uneducated alike. Nevertheless, the misspelling suggests lack of schooling, as the author intends it to do. The important point is that speaking and writing are essentially different.

In 1877 Samuel Clemens (Mark Twain) delivered a humorous speech telling an imaginary story of three great contemporary New England poets—Henry Wadsworth Longfellow, Ralph Waldo Emerson, and Oliver Wendell Holmes—spending a night in a miner's cabin in California. The three poets completely confuse the miner by reciting some of their poetry as if it were normal conversation. For instance, Holmes says:

> "Through the deep caves of thought
> I hear a voice that sings,
> Build thee more stately mansions,
> O my soul!"

The miner thinks that Holmes is telling him to build a more expensive house and replies, "I can't afford it, Mr. Holmes, and moreover I don't want to." The miner does not realize that Holmes is quoting written English rather than speaking to him. The humor of the speech lies in the confusion of spoken and written English.

The Speech

This is an occasion peculiarly meet for the digging up of pleasant reminiscences concerning literary folk; therefore I will drop lightly into history myself. Standing here on the shore of the Atlantic and contemplating certain of its largest literary billows, I am reminded of a thing which happened to me thirteen years ago, when I had just succeeded in stirring up a little Nevadian literary puddle myself, whose spume-flakes were beginning to blow thinly Californiaward. I started an inspection tramp through the southern mines of California. I was callow and conceited, and I resolved to try the virtue of my *nom de guerre.*[2]

I very soon had an opportunity. I knocked at a miner's lonely log cabin in the foot-hills of the Sierras just at nightfall. It was snowing at the time. A jaded, melancholy man of fifty, barefooted, opened the door to me. When he heard my *nom de guerre* he looked more dejected than before. He let me in—pretty reluctantly, I thought—and after the customary bacon and beans, black coffee and hot whiskey, I took a pipe. This sorrowful man had not said three words up to this time. Now he spoke up and said, in the voice of one who is secretly suffering, "You're the fourth—I'm going to move." "The fourth what?" said I. "The fourth literary man that has been here in twenty-four hours—I'm going to move." "You don't tell me!" said I; "Who were the others?" "Mr. Longfellow, Mr. Emerson, and Mr. Oliver Wendell Holmes—consound the lot!"

You can easily believe I was interested. I supplicated—three hot whiskies did the rest—and finally the melancholy miner began. Said he:

"They came here just at dark yesterday evening, and I let them in, of course. Said they were going to the Yosemite. They were a rough lot, but that's nothing; everybody looks rough that travels afoot. Mr. Emerson was a seedy little bit of a chap, redheaded. Mr. Holmes was as fat as a balloon; he weighed as much as three hundred, and had double chins all the way down to his stomach. Mr. Longfellow was built like a prize-fighter. His head was cropped and bristly, like as if he had a wig made of hairbrushes. His nose lay straight down his face, like a finger with the end joint tilted up. They had been drinking, I could see that. And what queer talk they used! Mr. Holmes inspected this cabin, then he took me by the buttonhole, and says he:

[2] *Nom de guerre:* pseudonym. Here the author refers to his pen name, Mark Twain.

" 'Through the deep caves of thought
I hear a voice that sings,
Build thee more stately mansions,
O my soul!'

"Says I, 'I can't afford it, Mr. Holmes, and moreover I don't want to.' Blamed if I liked it pretty well, either, coming from a stranger, that way. However, I started to get out my bacon and beans, when Mr. Emerson came and looked on awhile, and then *he* takes me aside by the buttonhole and says:

" 'Gives me agates for my meat;
Gives me cantharids to eat;
From air and ocean bring me foods,
From all zones and altitudes.'

"Says I, 'Mr. Emerson, if you'll excuse me, this ain't no hotel.' You see it sort of riled me—I warn't used to the ways of littery swells. But I went on a-sweating over my work, and next comes Mr. Longfellow and buttonholes me, and interrupts me. Says he:

" 'Honor be to Mudjekeewis!
You shall hear how Pau-Puk-Keewis—'

"But I broke in, and says I, 'Beg your pardon, Mr. Longfellow, if you'll be so kind as to hold your yawp for about five minutes and let me get this grub ready, you'll do me proud.' Well, sir, after they'd filled up I set out the jug. Mr. Holmes looks at it, and then he fires up all of sudden and yells:

" 'Flash out a stream of blood-red wine!
For I would drink to other days.'

"By George, I was getting kind of worked up. I don't deny it, I was getting kind of worked up. I turns to Mr. Holmes, and says I, 'Looky here, my fat friend, I'm a-running this shanty, and if the court knows herself, you'll take whisky straight or you'll go dry.' Them's the very words I said to him. Now I don't want to sass such famous littery people, but you see they kind of forced me. There ain't nothing onreasonable 'bout me; I don't mind a passel of guests a-treadin' on my tail three or four times, but when it comes to *standing* on it it's different, 'and if the court knows herself,' I says, 'you'll take whisky straight or you'll go dry.' Well, between drinks they'd swell around the cabin and strike attitudes and spout; and pretty soon they got out a greasy old deck and went to playing euchre[3] at ten cents a corner—on

[3] Euchre: a card game. In the game there is only one "right bower." There being two right bowers would mean that one of the players was cheating.

trust. I began to notice some pretty suspicious things. Mr. Emerson dealt, looked at his hand, shook his head, says:

> " 'I am the doubter and the doubt—'

and ca'mly bunched the hands and went to shuffling for a new layout. Says he:

> " 'They reckon ill who leave me out;
> They know not well the subtle ways I keep
> I pass and deal *again*!'

Hang'd if he didn't go ahead and do it, too! Oh, he was a cool one! Well, in about a minute things were running pretty tight, but all of a sudden I see by Mr. Emerson's eye he judged he had 'em. He had already corralled two tricks, and each of the others one. So now he kind of lifts a little in his chair and says:

> " 'I tire of globes and aces!—
> Too long the game is played!'

—and down he fetched a right bower. Mr. Longfellow smiles as sweet as pie and says:

> " 'Thanks thanks to thee, my worthy friend,
> For the lesson thou has taught,'

—and blamed if he didn't down with *another* right bower! Emerson claps his hand on his bowie, Longfellow claps his on his revolver, and I went under a bunk. There was going to be trouble; but that monstrous Holmes rose up, wobbling his double chins, and says he, 'Order, gentlemen; the first man that draws, I'll lay down on him and smother him!' All quiet on the Potomac, you bet!

"They were pretty how-come-you-so by now, and they begun to blow. Emerson says, 'The nobbiest thing I ever wrote was "Barbara Frietchie." ' Says Longfellow, 'It don't begin with my "Biglow Papers." ' Says Holmes, 'My "Thanatopsis" lays over 'em both.'[4] They mighty near ended in a fight. Then they wished they had some more company—and Mr. Emerson pointed to me and says:

> " 'Is yonder squalid peasant all
> That this proud nursery could breed?"

He was a-whetting his bowie on his boot—so I let it pass. Well, sir, next they took it into their heads that they would like some music; so they made me stand up and sing "When Johnny Comes Marching Home" till I dropped—at thirteen

[4] Here each poet claims authorship of another poet's work. Emerson claims Whittier's "Barbara Frietchie"; Longfellow claims Lowell's "Biglow Papers"; Holmes claims Bryant's "Thanatopsis."

minutes past four this morning. That's what I've been through, my friend. When I woke at seven, they were leaving, thank goodness, and Mr. Longfellow had my only boots on, and his'n under his arm. Says I, 'Hold on, there, Evangeline, what are you going to do with *them*?' He says, 'Going to make tracks with 'em; because:

> " 'Lives of great men all remind us
> We can make our lives sublime;
> And, departing, leave behind us
> Footprints on the sands of time.'

As I said, Mr. Twain, you are the fourth in twenty-four hours—and I'm going to move; I ain't suited to a littery atmosphere."

I said to the miner, "Why, my dear sir, *these* were not the gracious singers to whom we and the world pay loving reverence and homage; these were imposters."

The miner investigated me with a calm eye for awhile; then said he, "Ah! imposters, were they? Are *you*?"

I did not pursue the subject, and since then I have not traveled on my *nom de guerre* enough to hurt. Such was the reminiscence I was moved to contribute, Mr. Chairman. In my enthusiasm I may have exaggerated the details a little, but you will easily forgive me that fault, since I believe it is the first time I have ever deflected from perpendicular fact on an occasion like this.

Now look at this passage from Stephen Crane's *The Red Badge of Courage,* in which Crane describes a brigade of Civil War soldiers crouched in a grove of trees, watching the progress of a battle. The first three paragraphs represent the soldiers' nonstandard speech. The last paragraph is standard written English and Crane writes in his own person, using his vocabulary artistically to help us see the men and the battle more vividly. Notice the author's use of such phrases as "tremendous chorus," "frozen to silence," and such adjectives as "blurred," "agitated," and "turbulent." Here he omits all eye dialect, which he uses very freely in the soldiers' speech. Some of the big differences between speech and writing are clearly apparent in this passage.

"That young Hasbrouck, he makes a good off'cer. He ain't afraid 'a nothin'."

"I met one of th' 148th Maine boys an' he ses his brigade fit th' hull rebel army fer four hours over on th' turnpike road an' killed about five thousand of 'em. He ses one more sech fight as that an' th' war'll be over."

"Bill wasn't scared either. No, sir! It wasn't that. Bill ain't a-gittin' scared easy. He was jest mad, that's what he was. When that feller trod on his hand, he up an' sed that he was willin' t' give his hand t' his country, but he be dumbed if he was goin' t' have every dumb bushwacker in th' kentry walkin' 'round on it. So he went t' th' hospital disregardless of th' fight. Three fingers was crunched. Th' dern doctor wanted t' amputate 'm, an' Bill, he raised a heluva row, I hear. He' a funny feller."

The din in front swelled to a tremendous chorus. The youth and his fellows were frozen to silence. They could see a flag that tossed in the smoke angrily. Near it were the blurred and agitated forms of troops. There came a turbulent stream of men across the fields. A battery changing position at a frantic gallop scattered the stragglers right and left.

III. Standard–Nonstandard

Standard English is defined in *Webster's Third New International Dictionary* as

> . . . the English that with respect to spelling, grammar, pronunciation, and vocabulary is substantially uniform though not devoid of regional differences, that is well-established by usage in the formal and informal speech and writing of the educated, and that is widely recognized as acceptable wherever English is spoken and understood . . . .

Standard English differs from nonstandard English in pronunciation, vocabulary, and grammar. If a child speaks standard English, it is because standard English is spoken in his home. Similarly, the speaker of nonstandard English reflects the English spoken in his home. Children always learn to speak the kind of English they hear spoken around them.

In every English-speaking country both types of English exist. In 1916 George Bernard Shaw wrote, in *Pygmalion,* about the situation in England. Alan Jay Lerner adapted this play into a Broadway musical, *My Fair Lady.*

My Fair Lady opens with Professor Henry Higgins asking, "Why can't the English teach their children how to speak?" Eliza Doolittle, the Cockney flower girl, speaks the nonstandard language he hates. He thinks that "this verbal class distinction by now should be antique." He sings:

Look at her—a pris'ner of the gutters;
Condemned by ev'ry syllable she utters.
By right she should be taken out and hung
For the cold-blooded murder of the English tongue!*

Eliza exclaims, "Garn!" and Professor Higgins says to his friend Pickering:

I ask you, sir, what sort of word is that?
It's "Aooow" and "Garn" that keep her in her place.
Not her wretched clothes and dirty face. . . .
An Englishman's way of speaking absolutely classifies him. . . .
Why can't the English teach their children how to speak?
This verbal class distinction by now should be antique.*

In the United States also, a person's way of speaking classifies him. The contrast between standard and nonstandard English and the relation of both to life are clearly shown in Sherwood Anderson's story, "I'm a Fool." The boy telling the story speaks nonstandard English. He confesses that he has not graduated from high school and pretends that his lack of education does not matter. "A fellow just because he has been a swipe[5] with a race horse, and works taking care of horses for a man in the teaming, delivery, and storage business isn't any better or worse than any one else." However, he is very concerned with dressing well, he is thankful that his mother has taught him table manners, and his highest compliment for the girl he likes is "she could talk proper grammar without being like a schoolteacher or something like that." The boy himself, however, does not speak "proper grammar"—standard English. He uses many double negatives: "I knew enough not to do it in no bragging way"; "that couldn't never be made straight to a lady like her." He uses nonstandard past tense forms: "come" instead of *came,* "give" instead of *gave,* "says" instead of *said.* He also uses "hisself," "ain't," and "he don't."

The main story begins at three o'clock one October afternoon in the grandstand at the fall trotting and pacing meet in Sandusky, Ohio. During the previous autumn, the boy had worked as a swipe for Harry Whitehead, owner of two racehorses. On this job the boy learned about horses and horse racing from Burt, his fellow swipe and best friend—a big, kind,

---

[5] Swipe: One who rubs down horses.

skillful Negro. Together they groomed the Whitehead horses through the fall race meets and fairs. The boy loved this life, but his mother and sister thought being a swipe was disgraceful. To please them, he quit racehorses for good and found a job taking care of workhorses for the owner of a teaming, delivery, storage, coal, and real-estate business in Sandusky. The boy relates the story.

> And then, as I started to tell you, the fall races come to Sandusky and I got the day off and I went. I left the job at noon and had on my good clothes and my new brown derby hat I'd bought the Saturday before, and a stand-up collar.
>
> First of all I went downtown and walked about with the dudes. I've always thought to myself, Put up a good front, and so I did it. I had forty dollars in my pocket and so I went into the West House, a big hotel, and walked up to the cigar stand. "Give me three twenty-five-cent cigars," I said. There was a lot of horsemen and strangers and dressed-up people from other towns standing around in the lobby and in the bar, and I mingled amongst them. In the bar there was a fellow with a cane and a Windsor tie on, that it made me sick to look at him. I like a man to be a man and dress up, but not to go put on that kind of airs. So I pushed him aside, kind of rough, and had me a drink of whisky. And then he looked at me, as though he thought maybe he'd get gay, but he changed his mind and didn't say anything. And then I had another drink of whisky, just to show him something, and went out and had a hack out to the races, all to myself, and when I got there I bought myself the best seat I could get up in the grandstand, but didn't go in for any of these boxes. That's putting on too many airs.
>
> And so there I was, sitting up in the grandstand as gay as you please and looking down on the swipes coming out with their horses, and with their dirty horsey pants on and the horse blankets swung over their shoulders, same as I had been doing all the year before. I liked one thing about the same as the other, sitting up there and feeling grand and being down there and looking up at the yaps and feeling grander and more important, too. One thing's about as good as another, if you take it just right. I've often said that.
>
> Well, right in front of me, in the grandstand that day, there was a fellow with a couple of girls and they was about my age. The young fellow was a nice guy all right. He was the kind maybe that goes to college and then comes to be a lawyer or maybe a newspaper editor or something like that,

but he wasn't stuck on himself. There are some of that kind are all right and he was one of the ones.

He had his sister with him and another girl, and the sister looked around over his shoulder, accidental at first, not intending to start anything—she wasn't that kind—and her eyes and mine happened to meet.

You know how it is. Gee, she was a peach! She had on a soft dress, kind of a blue stuff and it looked carelessly made, but was well sewed and made and everything. I knew that much. I blushed when she looked right at me and so did she. She was the nicest girl I've ever seen in my life. She wasn't stuck on herself and she could talk proper grammar without being like a schoolteacher or something like that. What I mean is, she was O.K. I think maybe her father was well-to-do, but not rich to make her chesty because she was his daughter, as some are. Maybe he owned a drugstore or a dry-goods store in their home town, or something like that. She never told me and I never asked.

My own people are all O.K. too, when you come to that. My grandfather was Welsh and over in the old country, in Wales he was—But never mind that.

The first heat of the first race come off and the young fellow setting there with the two girls left them and went down to make a bet. I knew what he was up to, but he didn't talk big and noisy and let everyone around know he was a sport, as some do. He wasn't that kind. Well, he come back and I heard him tell the two girls what horse he'd bet on, and when the heat was trotted they all half got to their feet and acted in the excited, sweaty way people do when they've got money down on a race, and the horse they bet on is up there pretty close at the end, and they think maybe he'll come on with a rush, but he never does because he hasn't got the old juice in him, come right down to it.

And then, pretty soon, the horses came out for the 2:18 pace and there was a horse in it I knew. He was a horse Bob French had in his string but Bob didn't own him. He was a horse owned by a Mr. Mathers down at Marietta, Ohio.

This Mr. Mathers had a lot of money and owned some coal mines or something, and he had a swell place out in the country, and he was stuck on race horses, but was a Presbyterian or something, and I think more than likely his wife was one, too, maybe a stiffer one than himself. So he never raced his horses hisself, and the story round the Ohio race tracks was that when one of his horses got ready to go to the races he turned him over to Bob French and pretended to his wife he was sold.

So Bob had the horses and he did pretty much as he pleased and you can't blame Bob, at least I never did. Sometimes he was out to win and sometimes he wasn't. I never cared much about that when I was swiping a horse. What I did want to know was that my horse had the speed and could go out in front, if you wanted him to.

And, as I'm telling you, there was Bob in this race with one of Mr. Mathers' horses, was named "About Ben Ahem" or something like that, and was fast as a streak. He was a gelding and had a mark of 2:21, but could step in :08 or :09.

The boy knows these facts because he and Burt had visited Mr. Mathers' estate during the Marietta Fair the year before. A friend of Burt's, who worked for Mr. Mathers, had shown them through the elegant house while the family was at the fair. He had also shown them "About Ben Ahem," and Burt had stepped the horse a mile on Mr. Mathers' private track. The boy continues with the story.

I'm only telling you to get everything straight. At Sandusky, that afternoon I was at the fair, this young fellow with the two girls was fussed, being with the girls and losing his bet. You know how a fellow is that way. One of them was his girl and the other his sister. I had figured that out.

"Gee whizz," I says to myself, "I'm going to give him the dope."

He was mighty nice when I touched him on the shoulder. He and the girls were nice to me right from the start and clear to the end. I'm not blaming them.

And so he leaned back and I give him the dope on About Ben Ahem. "Don't bet a cent on this first heat because he'll go like an oxen hitched to a plow, but when the first heat is over go right down and lay on your pile." That's what I told him.

Well, I never saw a fellow treat anyone sweller. There was a fat man sitting beside the little girl, that had looked at me twice by this time, and I at her, and both blushing, and what did he do but have the nerve to turn and ask the fat man to get up and change places with me so I could set with his crowd.

Gee whizz, craps amighty. There I was. What a chump I was to go and get gay up there in the West House bar, and just because that dude was standing there with a cane and that kind of a necktie on, to go and get all balled up and drink that whisky, just to show off.

Of course she would know, me setting right beside her and letting her smell of my breath. I could have kicked myself right down out of that grandstand and all around that race track and made a faster record than most of the skates of horses they had there that year.

Because that girl wasn't any mutt of a girl. What wouldn't I have give right then for a stick of chewing gum to chew, or a lozenger, or some liquorice, or most anything. I was glad I had those twenty-five-cent cigars in my pocket and right away I give that fellow one and lit one myself. Then that fat man got up and we changed places and there I was, plunked right down beside her.

They introduced themselves and the fellow's best girl, he had with him, was named Miss Elinor Woodbury, and her father was a manufacturer of barrels from a place called Tiffin, Ohio. And the fellow himself was named Wilbur Wessen and his sister was Miss Lucy Wessen.

I suppose it was their having such swell names that got me off my trolley. A fellow, just because he has been a swipe with a race horse, and works taking care of horses for a man in the teaming, delivery and storage business, isn't any better or worse than anyone else. I've often thought that, and said it too.

But you know how a fellow is. There's something in that kind of nice clothes, and the kind of nice eyes she had, and the way she had looked at me, awhile before, over her brother's shoulder, and me looking back at her, and both of us blushing.

I couldn't show her up for a boob, could I?

I made a fool of myself, that's what I did. I said my name was Walter Mathers from Marietta, Ohio, and then I told all three of them the smashingest lie you ever heard. What I said was that my father owned the horse About Ben Ahem and that he had let him out to this Bob French for racing purposes, because our family was proud and had never gone into racing that way, in our own name, I mean. Then I had got started and they were all leaning over and listening, and Miss Lucy Wessen's eyes were shining, and I went the whole hog.

I told about our place down at Marietta, and about the big stables and the grand brick house we had on a hill, up above the Ohio River, but I knew enough not to do it in no bragging way. What I did was to start things and then let them drag the rest out of me. I acted just as reluctant to tell as I could. Our family hasn't got any barrel factory, and since I've known us, we've always been pretty poor, but not asking anything of any one at that, and my grandfather, over in Wales—but never mind that.

We set there talking like we had known each other for years and years, and I went and told them that my father had been expecting maybe this Bob French wasn't on the square, and had sent me up to Sandusky on the sly to find out what I could.

And I bluffed it through I had found out all about the 2:18 pace, in which About Ben Ahem was to start.

I said he would lose the first heat by pacing like a lame cow and then he would come back and skin 'em alive after that. And to back up what I said I took thirty dollars out of my pocket and handed it to Mr. Wilbur Wessen and asked him, would he mind, after the first heat, to go down and place it on About Ben Ahem for whatever odds he could get. What I said was that I didn't want Bob French to see me and none of the swipes.

Sure enough the first heat come off and About Ben Ahem went off his stride, up the back stretch, and looked like a wooden horse or a sick one, and come in to be last. Then this Wilbur Wessen went down to the betting place under the grandstand and there I was with the two girls, and when that Miss Woodbury was looking the other way once, Lucy Wessen kinda, with her shoulder you know, kinda touched me. Not just tucking down, I don't mean. You know how a woman can do. They get close, but not getting gay either. You know what they do. Gee whizz.

And then they give me a jolt. What they had done, when I didn't know, was to get together, and they had decided Wilbur Wessen would bet fifty dollars, and the two girls had gone and put in ten dollars each, of their own money, too. I was sick then, but I was sicker later.

About the gelding, About Ben Ahem, and their winning their money, I wasn't worried a lot about that. It come out O.K. Ahem stepped the next three heats like a bushel of spoiled eggs going to market before they could be found out, and Wilbur Wessen had got nine to two for the money. There was something else eating at me.

Because Wilbur come back, after he had bet the money, and after that he spent most of his time talking to that Miss Woodbury, and Lucy Wessen and I was left alone together like on a desert island. Gee, if I'd only been on the square or if there had been any way of getting myself on the square. There ain't any Walter Mathers, like I said to her and them, and there hasn't ever been one, but if there was, I bet I'd go to Marietta, Ohio, and shoot him tomorrow.

There I was, big boob that I am. Pretty soon the race was over, and Wilbur had gone down and collected our money, and we had a hack downtown, and he stood us a swell supper at the West House, and a bottle of champagne beside.

And I was with that girl and she wasn't saying much, and I wasn't saying much either. One thing I know. She wasn't stuck on me because of the lie about my father being rich and all that. There's a way you know . . . . Craps amighty. There's a kind of girl, you see just once in your life, and if you don't get busy and make hay, then you're gone for good and all, and might as well go jump off a bridge. They give you a look from inside of them somewhere, and it ain't no vamping, and what it means is—you want that girl to be your wife, and you want nice things around her like flowers and swell clothes, and you want her to have the kids you're going to have, and you want good music played and no ragtime. Gee whizz.

There's a place over near Sandusky, across a kind of bay, and it's called Cedar Point. And after we had supper we went over to it in a launch, all by ourselves. Wilbur and Miss Lucy and that Miss Woodbury had to catch a ten-o'clock train back to Tiffin, Ohio, because, when you're out with girls like that you can't get careless and miss any trains and stay out all night, like you can with some kinds of Janes.

And Wilbur blowed himself to the launch and it cost him fifteen cold plunks, but I wouldn't never have knew if I hadn't listened. He wasn't no tin horn kind of a sport.

Over at the Cedar Point place, we didn't stay around where there was a gang of common kind of cattle at all.

There was big dance halls and dining places for yaps, and there was a beach you could walk along and get where it was dark, and we went there.

She didn't talk hardly at all and neither did I, and I was thinking how glad I was my mother was all right, and always made us kids learn to eat with a fork at table, and not swill soup, and not be noisy and rough like a gang you see around a race track that way.

Then Wilbur and his girl went away up the beach and Lucy and I sat down in a dark place, where there was some roots of old trees the water had washed up, and after that the time, till we had to go back in the launch and they had to catch their trains, wasn't nothing at all. It went like winking your eye.

Here's how it was. The place we were setting in was dark, like I said, and there was the roots from that old stump sticking up like arms, and there was a watery smell, and the night was like—as if you could put your hand out and feel it—so warm and soft and dark and sweet like an orange.

I most cried and I most swore and I most jumped up and danced, I was so mad and happy and sad.

When Wilbur come back from being alone with his girl, and she saw him coming, Lucy she says, "We got to go to the train now," and she was most crying too, but she never knew nothing I knew, and she couldn't be so all busted up. And then, before Wilbur and Miss Woodbury got up to where we was, she put her face up and kissed me quick and put her head up against me and she was all quivering and—Gee whizz.

Sometimes I hope I have cancer and die. I guess you know what I mean. We went in the launch across the bay to the train like that, and it was dark, too. She whispered and said it was like she and I could get out of the boat and walk on the water, and it sounded foolish, but I knew what she meant.

And then quick we were right at the depot, and there was a big gang of yaps, the kind that goes to the fairs, and crowded and milling around like cattle, and how could I tell her? "It won't be long because you'll write and I'll write to you." That's all she said.

I got a chance like a hay barn afire. A swell chance I got.

And maybe she would write me, down at Marietta that way, and the letter would come back, and stamped on the front of it by the U.S.A. "there ain't any such guy," or something like that, whatever they stamp on a letter that way.

And me trying to pass myself off for a bigbug and a swell—to her, as decent a little body as God ever made. Craps amighty—a swell chance I got!

And then the train come in, and she got on it, and Wilbur Wessen, he come and shook hands with me, and that Miss Woodbury was nice too and bowed to me, and I at her, and the train went and I busted out and cried like a kid.

Gee, I could have run after that train and made Dan Patch look like a freight train after a wreck but, socks amighty, what was the use? Did you ever see such a fool?

I'll bet you what—if I had an arm broke right now or a train had run over my foot—I wouldn't go to no doctor at all. I'd go set down and let her hurt and hurt—that's what I'd do.

I'll bet you what—if I hadn't a drunk that booze I'd a never been such a boob as to go tell such a lie—that couldn't never be made straight to a lady like her.

> I wish I had that fellow right here that had on a Windsor tie and carried a cane. I'd smash him for fair. Gosh darn his eyes. He's a big fool—that's what he is.
>
> And if I'm not another you just go find me one and I'll quit working and be a bum and give him my job. I don't care nothing for working, and earning money, and saving it for no such boob as myself.
>
> From "I'm a Fool"
> by Sherwood Anderson.

IV. Formal–Informal–Technical

Formal. Formal English is the language of custom, ceremony, ritual, and law. Much less flexible than informal English, it is characterized by unchangeable phrasings and is not a regular part of normal conversation. Nevertheless, we use formal English frequently. After being introduced to someone, we usually say, "How do you do?" or, "I'm pleased to meet you." We do not expect the recipient of our greeting to tell us how he does. In fact we would be astonished if he did. Furthermore, we are not always certain that we are pleased to meet him. We have simply gone through the necessary formalities of an introduction.

Oath-taking also involves formal English. The language of marriage vows, the pledge of allegiance to the flag, the swearing-in of court witnesses, and the induction oath of the armed services are among many examples of formal English reserved for serious occasions. Words and ceremony are in these circumstances virtually inseparable. The substitution of informal English in a wedding ceremony, for instance, would violate the sanctity of the occasion, in most people's eyes; the use of this kind of formal language without the customary formal trappings would, on the other hand, appear ludicrous.

Although formal language often tends to be high-sounding and precise, it is not always so. Nor is its use restricted to educated speakers. Proverbs are fixed, formal statements used by educated and uneducated alike. "A stitch in time saves nine" conveys the same general meaning to almost all native speakers of our language and would be no more surprising in the speech of an unschooled mountaineer than in that of a professor.

Informal. The line between formal and informal English is blurred; there are bound to be loopholes in any description of one or the other. Nevertheless it is safe to observe that most of our speech is informal; and that much of our writing falls into the same category. Conversation is by nature informal—in the speech of even the most highly educated people, contractions, uncompleted sentences, "ah's" and "uh-huh's" are the rule, not the exception. And while we may consciously attempt to "formalize" our writing in tests, compositions, and letters to prospective employers, we would most likely lapse into a more comfortable informality in a journal, a personal essay, or a letter to a friend. (There is nothing wrong, by the way, with informal written English. Used appropriately, it is most effective.)

Below is a transcript of standard informal spoken English. On their office telephones, two university professors are discussing typewriters. One phone has been hooked up to a tape recorder, which records their conversation. One professor does most of the talking. The other says only the words in parentheses. These words serve as a kind of oral punctuation; there is no written punctuation.

> I wanted to tell you one more thing I've been talking with Mr. D_____ in the purchasing department about our typewriter (yes) that order went in March seventh however it seems that we are about eighth on the list (I see) we were up about three but it seems that for that type of typewriter we're about eighth that's for a fourteen-inch carriage with pica type (I see) now he told me that R_____'s have in stock the fourteen-inch carriage typewriters with elite type (oh) and elite type varies sometimes it's quite small and sometimes it's almost as large as pica (yes I know) he suggested that we go down and get Mrs. R_____ and tell her who we are and that he sent us and try the fourteen-inch typewriters and see if our stencils would work with such type (I see) and if we can use them to get them right away because they have those in stock and we won't have to wait (that's right) we're short one typewriter right now as far as having adequate facilities for the staff is concerned (yes) we're short and we want to get rid of those rentals (that's right) but they are expecting within two weeks or so to be receiving—ah—to start receiving their orders on eleven-inch machines with pica type (oh) and of course pica type has always been best for our stencils (yes) but I rather think there might be a chance that we can work with elite type (well you go over and try them and see what they're like and do that as soon as you can so that we'll not miss our chance at these.)[6]

[6] Charles Carpenter Fries, *The Structure of English*. New York: Harcourt, Brace and World, Inc., 1952, pp. 50-51.

If we edited this conversation into written form, we would add punctuation, capital letters, and indentions. We would subtract some of the *and*'s as well as the false start, "to be receiving—ah—." The result would be standard informal written English.

Slang is an extremely informal use of language. Most slang expressions move in and out of the language quickly, but a few become permanent parts of English. In "I'm a Fool" we can see many examples of dated slang—that is, slang that was popular when Sherwood Anderson originally wrote the story in 1924. Here are some examples with their modern meanings:

". . . there was a big gang of *yaps* . . ." (*Yap* is a scornful term for *man.*) "Because that girl wasn't any *mutt* of a girl." (*Mutt* is a shortened form of *muttonhead.*) "I think maybe her father was well-to-do, but not rich to make her *chesty* because she was his daughter. . . ." (*Chesty* here means *conceited.*) "What a *chump* I was to go . . . and get *all balled up.* . . ." (*Chump* means *fool. All balled up* means *completely confused.*) "They give you a look from inside of them somewhere, and it ain't no *vamping.* . . ." (*Vamping* means *flirting.*) ". . . it cost him fifteen *cold plunks.* . . ." (*Cold plunks* means *hard dollars.*) "He wasn't no *tin horn* kind of a *sport.*" (*Tin horn sport* means *cheap fellow.*)

Technical. Each field of human activity has a specific vocabulary for discussing the subjects with which it deals. For instance, in this book you will become further acquainted with the technical vocabulary needed to discuss English. Here are some of the technical words of horse racing used in "I'm a Fool":

Heat: a single division of a race.

Swipe: one who rubs down horses.

Pace: a two-beat gait in which the legs move in lateral pairs and support the horse alternately on the right and left legs.

Trot: a gait in which the horse's legs move in diagonal pairs.

Back stretch: the side opposite the homestretch on a race course.

Here are some technical words from the language of skiers.[7]

Basher: a fast skier. Occasionally, a reckless skier, or a fast skier who loses control.

Comma position: a position in which the body is curved to the side and assumes the shape of a comma or half-moon.

[7] Horst Jarka, "The Language of Skiers," *American Speech,* XXXVIII (October 1963) pp. 202-208.

Plant the pole: to set in the pole ahead of one so as to pivot around it in making a turn.

Royal Christie: a skid turn with the skis mostly parallel, executed on one ski while the other is off the ground.

Shoot an avalanche: to release an avalanche with explosives in order to prevent an accident.

Ski bum: a ski enthusiast who goes from one ski area to another taking odd jobs just for the sake of skiing.

Snow ranger: a U.S. Forest Service employee responsible for the safety of skiers in National Forest areas.

In addition, here are some slang terms from the language of skiers.

Dope slope: a beginners' slope. Also called *Nursery* or *Nursery Slope.*

Double dipsies or *Double doodles:* a series of short parallel turns close to the fall line.

Eggbeater: a bad fall in which the skier usually turns head over skis and swirls up a cloud of snow.

Ski bunny: a beginner, usually a female.

Trail hog: a skier who takes up all the space on a narrow trail.

Here are some technical words from the vocabulary of air refueling, the mid-air transfer of fuel from a tanker aircraft to a receiver aircraft.[8]

Buddy refueling: a refueling technique by which the tanker and the receiver take off and fly together until the receiver is ready to accept fuel from the tanker.

Head-on refueling: a refueling technique whereby the tanker and receiver fly toward one another and at a computed time the tanker makes a 180 degree turn and the receiver then moves up behind for refueling.

Point refueling: a refueling technique whereby the tanker orbits at a specified geographical point and then departs for another designated point, planning to arrive there simultaneously with the receiver.

Parrot: an electronic device in an aircraft that makes a distinctive mark on the ground radar scope.

Strangle the parrot: turn off the parrot.

Porpoise: an undesired landing in which the aircraft on the runway bobs up and down like a porpoise on the waves.

In addition, here are some slang words from the vocabulary of air refueling.

Air sucker: a jet aircraft.

In the green: an expression meaning that all instruments show safe readings.

Mole hole: the alert barracks where the alert crews live. Most such buildings are underground and windowless and have tunnels running up to the surface.

Bird dog: a navigational instrument that points in the direction of any radio station tuned in on it.

V. Northern–Midland–Southern

After listening to the speech of a native Britisher, we might conclude that he talked "funny." Not only would his pronunciation be different from ours, but he would also include in his speech a number of strange terms, such as *lorry* for truck, *chemist* for druggist, *lift* for elevator. Although English is the most

[8] Thomas Stell Newman, "Air Refueling Words," *American Speech*, XXXVIII (May 1963), pp. 117-120.

widely used language in the world, it is largely a creature of *place*. In our own country as well as others, people from different places use different terms and different pronunciations.

John Steinbeck traveled with his dog Charley from Long Island to Maine, and then across the United States to the Pacific Ocean, to Texas, and then home again to New York. We can go with him and listen to the people of the United States speak in his book *Travels with Charley in Search of America*. Of the New Englander he says:

> The farmer was a spare man, with what we think of as a Yankee face and the flat vowels we consider Yankee pronunciation.

When he reaches Texas he recalls his wife's speech because "you would not have to scratch very deep to find her origin"; she was raised in Texas.

> She says such words as yes, air, hair, guess, with two syllables —yayus, ayer, hayer, gayus. And sometimes in a weary moment the word ink becomes ank. Our daughter, after a stretch in Austin, was visiting New York friends. She said, "Do you have a pin?"
>
> "Certainly, dear," said her host. "Do you want a straight pin or a safety pin?"
>
> "Aont a fountain pin," she said.

In Montana, Steinbeck says:

> Here for the first time I heard a definite regional accent unaffected by TV-ese, a slow-paced warm speech.

Dialect is the technical word for what Steinbeck calls "accent." A regional dialect is a particular type of speech that is used in a definite geographical location, and that differs from other regional dialects in pronunciation, vocabulary, and grammar.

In the United States there are three main dialect areas—Northern, Midland, and Southern. These three areas are marked by the ways people pronounce words, name things, and construct their sentences. These differences are never big enough to block communication. John Steinbeck's daughter, for instance, will eventually get a fountain pen.

As H. L. Mencken says in *The American Language:*

> The differences in pronunciation between American dialects seldom impede free communication, for a man who converts *pass* into *pahs* or drops the final *r* in *father* is still usually able

> to palaver readily with one who gives *pass* the *a* of *Dan* and wrings the last gurgle out of his *r*'s. The differences in vocabulary are sometimes more puzzling, but they are not very numerous, and a stranger quickly picks them up. A newcomer to Maryland soon abandons *faucet,* or *tap,* or whatever it was that prevailed in his native wilds, and turns easily to the local *spigot.* In the same way an immigrant to the Deep South is rapidly fluent in the use of *you-all, yonder,* and *to carry* in the sense of to convey. Even the differences in intonation are much less marked between any two parts of the United States than they are between any two parts of England, or than between England and this country as a whole. The railroad, the automobile, the mail-order catalogue, the movie, and above all, radio and television have promoted uniformity in even the most remote backwaters.

Here is a poem by Sidney Lanier, "Thar's More in the Man Than Thar Is in the Land," showing the regional dialect of Georgia as spoken by an uneducated farmer. Certain key words label the dialect both Southern and nonstandard: *boughten* instead of *bought, riz* instead of *rose, mought* instead of *might, driv* instead of *drove, tuck* instead of *took, see* instead of *saw, sot* instead of *sat* or *set,* for examples. The rhymes help us to know how to pronounce the words that are misspelled to give the sound, sense, and swing of the dialect.

Thar's More in the Man Than Thar Is in the Land

I knowed a man, which he lived in Jones,
Which Jones is a country of red hills and stones,
And he lived pretty much by gittin' of loans,
And his mules was nuthin' but skin and bones,
And his hogs was flat as his corn-bread pones, 5
And he had 'bout a thousand acres o' land.

This man—which his name it was also Jones—
He swore that he'd leave them old red hills and stones,
Fur he couldn't make nuthin' but yallerish cotton,
And little o' *that,* and his fences was rotten, 10
And what little corn he had, *hit* was boughten
And dinged ef a livin' was in the land.

And the longer he swore the madder he got,
And he riz and he walked to the stable lot,
And he hollered to Tom to come thar and hitch 15
Fur to emigrate somewhar whar land was rich,
And to quit raisin' cock-burrs, thistles and sich,
And a wastin' ther time on the cussed land.

So him and Tom they hitched up the mules,
Pertestin' that folks was mighty big fools 20
That 'ud stay in Georgy ther lifetime out,
Jest scratchin' a livin' when all of 'em mought
Git places in Texas whar cotton would sprout
By the time you could plant it in the land.

And he driv by a house whar a man named Brown 25
Was a livin', not fur from the edge o' town,
And he bantered Brown fur to buy his place,
And said that bein' as money was skace,
And bein' as sheriffs was hard to face,
Two dollars an acre would git the land. 30

They closed at a dollar and fifty cents,
And Jones he bought him a waggin and tents,
And loaded his corn, and his wimmin, and truck,
And moved to Texas, which it tuck
His entire pile, with the best of luck, 35
To git thar and git him a little land.

But Brown moved out on the old Jones' farm,
And he rolled up his breeches and bared his arm,
And he picked all the rocks from off'n the groun',
And he rooted it up and he plowed it down, 40
Then he sowed his corn and his wheat in the land.

Five years glid by, and Brown, one day
(Which he'd got so fat that he wouldn't weigh),
Was a settin' down, sorter lazily,
To the bulliest dinner you ever see, 45
When one o' the children jumped on his knee
And says, "Yon's Jones, which you bought his land."

And thar was Jones, standin' out at the fence,
And he hadn't no waggin, nor mules, nor tents,
Fur he had left Texas afoot and cum 50
To Georgy to see if he couldn't git sum
Employment, and he was lookin' as hum-
Ble as ef he had never owned any land.

But Brown he axed him in, and he sot
Him down to his vittles smokin' hot, 55
And when he had filled hisself and the floor
Brown looked at him sharp and riz and swore
That, "whether men's land was rich or poor
Thar was more in the man than thar was in the land."

Summary. To make these five language dimensions easier to observe and discuss, we have presented them in isolation. But that is not the way they exist and work as language. In the dialogue from *Flower Drum Song,* other variables work together with the time dimension of the two generations. Both of the generations are speaking informal English, but the children's slang is much more informal than the parents' language. Therefore, in addition to showing the old-young contrast, the song illustrates the formal-informal dimension.

Although the Mark Twain speech showed the contrast between spoken and written English, it also shows the formal-informal dimension. In addition to that, it shows the geographic dimension. The three poets communicate in standard, formal, written, New England usage and the miner speaks nonstandard, informal, California dialect.

Of course, every time we speak to a person who is older, younger, or the same age as we are, we do not ask ourselves, "Shall I speak standard or nonstandard, Northern, Midland, or Southern English?" We just talk, making nearly automatic adjustments to fit the circumstances. But our awareness of these variables could help us analyze a situation in which communication had failed or succeeded. More important, perhaps, it provides a partial answer to the question, *What is Language?*

Exercise one. Here are five selections illustrating the five dimensions of American English combined in interesting ways. With the help of the accompanying comments and questions, analyze each selection to discover these dimensions and how they interweave in each selection.

1. This is an excerpt from *Up the Down Staircase* by Bel Kaufman. It is a love letter written by a young high school student to her English teacher. He has marked her letter as if it were a theme. Because of his answer to her letter, she attempts suicide. How well has the teacher coped with the young-old dimension of American English in

bridging the communication gap between himself and the girl? What extra complications are added to the situation by her use of writing instead of speech? Later, the teacher asks an associate how she would have handled a love letter from a student. How would you answer his question?

Dear Mr. Barringer,

Last Sunday I took the subway to your stop having looked it up on your Time Card. I hope you don't mind the presumtion ..... I walked back and forth across the street from your house back and forth .. and I thought I saw you and my heart was throbbing with this love I bear for you..

I feel so deeply the Beauty and Truth of the poetry you read in class I alone.. especially such lines like "She has a lovely face, the Lady of Shalot....."

I think of you all the time .. at night, darkling, I pray to be worthy of you and all that you stand for..... I believe we understand each other and no one else ..... And if ever you need me to die for you I will gladly do so......

I hope you don't think me presumtious but I have to speak out the truth .. the only truth ..

Sincerely yours,
Alice Blake

Alice—
Thank you for your note. Watch spelling and punctuation; you tend to use a series of dots to avoid it! Watch repetitions and clichés.
You might look up the spelling of the Lady in Tennyson's "Idylls of the King"—
P.B.

2. This selection is from Jesse Stuart's *Hie to the Hunters,* a story of the Kentucky mountains, where Midland dialect is spoken. Didway, a wealthy city boy, and Sparkie, a poor country boy, are true friends. But Sparkie's mother remarks of Did, "He's not our people. He talks so funny!" She gets this answer from her husband, "He talks proper. City folks talk proper! They don't talk like us. That proper talk is quaire to us." In the excerpt Sparkie urges Did

to come home with him to his hill shack. Compare the speech of the two boys as they discuss the plan. Which dimensions of American English appear here in addition to the geographic? Cite specific examples to support your answer.

"See, this is my second year in Greenwood High School and Mother and Father wouldn't let me quit," Did apologized. "I'd have to run away from home if I went with you."

"Ye're high up in larnin'," Sparkie said. "To look at ye, one wouldn't think it."

"Don't you go to school, Sparkie?"

"I ust to. I got to the Second Reader; then I quit."

"What do you do now?"

"I hep Peg a little with the terbacker patchin'. I hunt, trap, go to a few dances."

"Have you got hound-dogs?"

"I got four left. I had four pizened by the terbacker men."

"Why?"

"Because they run the foxes through their green terbacker, uprootin' it and a-breakin' the ground leaves. Ye see why I'm on the dogs' side. Drive, Lead, Topper, and Scout got pizened on fried taters; but I got four left—Shootin' Star, Lightnin', Fleet, and Thunderbolt."

"Have you got a gun?"

"Couple of shotguns and two pistols!"

Did stood for a minute in silence. He looked thoughtfully at Sparkie.

"Will you teach me to hunt and shoot if I go home with you?"

"I'll shore larn ye."

From *Hie to the Hunters*
by Jesse Stuart.

3. Here is another conversation between Jesse Stuart's Did and Sparkie. Explain how this passage illustrates the formal-informal dimension as well as the old-young, standard-nonstandard, and geographic dimensions.

   As the two boys approach the cabin, Did says, "That wood smoke smells good."

"It ain't all wood smoke ye smell," Sparkie told him. "Ye're a-smellin' vittles cookin'. Arn's gettin' supper."

"Who's Arn?"

"That's Ma," Sparkie said, staring strangely at Did.

I couldn't call my mother by her first name, Did thought. She wouldn't stand that a minute. Did had always called his mother "Mother" and his father "Father." They wouldn't even let him call them Mom and Pop, and certainly not by their first names.

"Before we go inside the shack and meet Arn and Peg," Sparkie said, "I want to take you out here and interduce you to the best hound-dogs in these hills."

4. Here is a conversation among three speakers in Harper Lee's *To Kill a Mockingbird.* The first speaker is Calpurnia, the Negro housekeeper and trusted helper of the widowed attorney, Atticus Finch of Finches Landing, Alabama. Calpurnia is guide and mentor to Atticus Finch's two motherless children: the boy, Jem, and the little girl, Jean Louise, nicknamed "Scout." Jem and Scout are the two other speakers. Calpurnia served the children's grandparents and was educated by them through reading the *Commentaries* of Sir William Blackstone, a great English jurist of the eighteenth century. Calpurnia speaks standard English with the Finches. However, she shifts to nonstandard English when she takes the children to visit her church and Scout notices that Calpurnia is speaking unnaturally. Scout says, "I thought her voice strange: she was talking like the rest of them." Calpurnia and her son, Zeebo, are two of only four persons in the congregation who can read. Calpurnia taught Zeebo to read by means of Blackstone's *Commentaries,* too.

In the conversation Scout is the narrator. What are the two "languages" Calpurnia commands? Remembering that Calpurnia, Jem, and Scout speak standard English, how do you explain Scout's using the nonstandard term *nigger-talk?* How does Calpurnia refer to the speech of her "folks"? What is Calpurnia's responsibility as teacher to small Scout? Is she perhaps quietly rebuking Scout for not being "ladylike"? In terms of the spoken-written dimension of American English, how accurate are the spellings *outa, 'em, hafta, puttin', knowin', gonna,* and *talkin',* compared to the actual pronunciation of these words in informal conversation?

That Calpurnia led a modest double life never dawned on me. The idea that she had a separate existence outside our household was a novel one, to say nothing of her having command of two languages.

"Cal," I asked "why do you talk nigger-talk to the—to your folks when you know it's not right?"

"Well, in the first place I'm black—"

"That doesn't mean you hafta talk that way when you know better," said Jem.

Calpurnia tilted her hat and scratched her head, then pressed her hat down carefully over her ears. "It's right hard to say," she said. "Suppose you and Scout talked colored-folks' talk at home—it'd be out of place, wouldn't it? Now what if I talked white-folks' talk at church, and with my neighbors? They'd think I was puttin' on airs to beat Moses."

"But, Cal, you know better," I said.

"It's not necessary to tell all you know. It's not ladylike—in the second place, folks don't like to have somebody around knowin' more than they do. It aggravates 'em. You're not gonna change any of them by talkin' right, they've got to want to learn themselves, and when they don't want to learn there's nothing you can do but keep your mouth shut or talk their language."

From *To Kill a Mockingbird*
by Harper Lee.

5. In the following selection from Sterling North's *So Dear to My Heart,* Jeremiah Kincaid, an Indiana backwoods boy, shows his black lamb, Dan Patch II, at the County Fair. All through this ordeal, Jerry finds courage and comfort in the Twenty-third Psalm. Contrast the formal prayer language of the psalm with Jerry's normal conversational language. Jerry speaks Midland dialect. What other dimensions of American English does the story illustrate?

Now Jeremiah was on his own. In the whole world there was only himself and his lamb walking into that frightening place of judgment. He knew now how the Christian martyrs felt when they went forth into the Roman arena. He needed the aid of someone stronger than himself. He knew he had the love of Granny and Uncle Hiram and Tildy, but it was somehow not enough.

"S'pose he don't win," he whispered to Granny as they parted.

"Happen he don't, I want you to come out of that ring like a Kincaid—walkin' proud."

One foot preceded the other the way they must even on Judgment Day, the lamb followed meekly on his tether. Jerry found himself repeating the opening words of the Twenty-third Psalm, his lips barely moving:

"The Lord is my Shepherd; I shall not want . . ."

He had to hold the leash tightly now, for Danny had found an adversary and playmate in a handsome white snub-nosed

Shropshire led by another Pike County boy. The young rams butted playfully, leaped in the air, whirled in the mad excitement of pretended anger.

The three judges, also making their way to the arena, laughed at the mischievous sporting lambs.

"Mighty handsome Shropshire," said one of the judges, "but that black rascal. I wonder . . ."

Their voices were lost in the noise of the crowd, but Jerry's heart sank in his bosom as he led his lamb along. His beloved Danny was of no breed one could name. Just betwixt and between, a common crossbred sheep of the backwoods variety. What chance did Danny have against these handsome purebred Shropshires, Hampshires, and American Merinos?

"He maketh me to lie down in green pastures:

"He leadeth me beside the still waters.

"He restoreth my soul . . ."

The judging ring was dotted with lambs, each with a handler kneeling beside his entry held on close tether. Jerry kneeled too, his heart beating wildly. Directly behind him along the rail were Granny, Tildy, Uncle Hiram, and the stranger. They would not forsake him in his hour of need. He took some comfort from the appearance of the judges: big men with just but kindly faces; the head judge tall and gravely serious.

As the trio moved from contestant to contestant, the owner's name was called:

"Holloway!" said the leading judge, consulting his clip sheet.

"Johnson County," replied the boy.

"Name of your entry?"

"Holloway's Hampshire. Number six nine two. Out of Midas the Second's Butter Cup Belle, by Crenshaw, Duke of Manchester."

There was a ripple of applause. Jeremiah's heart plummeted. How could Danny hope to match a lamb of such aristocratic lineage?

"Marshall!"

"Pike County."

The applause was deafening. There stood the well-groomed, snub-nosed Shropshire whom the judges had admired when Danny and he were jousting in the areaway. Both owner and ram were obviously popular.

"Name of your entry?"

"Shropshire Lad. Number seven eight seven four. Out of Lassie Queen, by National Grand Champion, Hiram of Troy's Golden Thorn."

Again the burst of applause for the boy and his beautifully fleeced Shropshire. Down the line of young men with their rams came the judges, calling out the names; receiving the proud answers. Jerry looked around him in panic. Yes, there were the only faces he knew in the crowd: Granny with new hat awry, yearning toward him; Tildy with lips slightly apart and cheeks burning with excitement; Hiram chewing nervously on an unlit cigar; and finally the amiable stranger who seemed to radiate confidence.

"Kincaid!"

No answer.

"Kincaid! Come, come, speak up!"

"Pike County," Jeremiah said in a small voice.

"Name of your entry?"

"Dan Patch II."

"What breed, boy? Rambouillet?"

The Twenty-third Psalm was still running through Jeremiah's mind (the words both comforting and gently exacting): "He leadeth me in the paths of righteousness for His Name's sake."

"What breed, son?"

Every eye in the great circle of faces was upon him. "Paths of righteousness." Jerry suddenly knew what the phrase meant. Granny would have to tell them the bitter truth about Danny. He had no right even to let them think he was a Rambouillet or any other pedigreed variety.

"Tell them, Granny," he called to the old woman leaning toward him over the rail.

"You tell them, son. Hold up yore head now!"

Jerry rose from his knees and stood very straight beside his lamb. "This black lamb of mine ain't no fancy purebred," he said in a proud, clear voice. "He's jest a Cat Hollow Kincaid, same as me and Granny."

The crowd was so quiet you could hear the far-away music of the merry-go-round.

"His mam's name was Jezebel. And we ain't quite sure who his pap was."

The crowd burst into raucous laughter.

"Go ahead, laugh," Jeremiah shouted, fighting back the tears. "But he's the best lamb in the world. He ain't afeared of nothin' or nobody. He got lost and he got found again. And he could lick all of these fancy rams any day in the week—like, like David licked Goliath."

The crowd howled with laughter. Men slapped each other on the back and roared. The tall chief judge held up his hand for silence, and said very clearly so that all could hear:

"Nice pair of shoulders on your lamb, my boy. Good quality wool too."

"Yea, though I walk through the Valley of the Shadow of Death I will fear no evil . . ." continued the voice in Jeremiah's mind.

The judges were in conference now, huddled together examining their notebooks. There were no red ribbons nor white ribbons in this particular event. And Jerry knew that in this hard world being second or third meant nothing. His lips were dry and he felt light-headed and a little sick—waiting—waiting.

What could be taking them so long? Time hung suspended like a great hawk over the breathless arena. The sun blazed down on the dusty grass, sending up little heat waves; the pennants drooped in defeat upon the still air. Although Jerry's throat and chest were so constricted he could scarcely breathe, he had a sense of seeing everything with the utmost clarity. Never before had he noticed the fine network of delicate veins in the translucent wings of the dragonfly, nor how its burnished colors change from bronze to purple to peacock blue. Was it good luck that for a moment this gleaming insect (astray from nearby marshes) lit on the tip of Danny's small left horn?

Minutes seemed hours while the judges argued. Jerry felt he could almost read their thoughts as he was trying to read their lips. Surely it was Holloway's Hampshire or Marshall's Shropshire Lad. Both boys were doubtless sons of fathers who were themselves breeders of sheep. They had been born and schooled to raise prize-winning lambs, could choose their entries from great flocks of purebred animals.

And yet a sudden flickering hope sprang up in his heart like the welcome breeze now fluttering the pennants. The Lord God Almighty had fashioned his black lamb; the same Creator who had made the birds of the air and the flowers of the field. What human could improve upon the works of the Almighty? He who with no help of man brought forth each spring the redbud and the mountain laurel, who taught the whippoorwill to sing and the oriole to build its nest.

"God don't need nobody's help," Jeremiah whispered to his lamb. He felt a new fierce pride in Danny's ebony perfection. A Greater Shepherd than Holloway or Marshall had helped Jeremiah raise a winner. A Greater Judge than those three men in conference would confer the prize.

But Jerry's new-found courage faced a bitter test as the judges, nodding solemnly, turned to make the awards. Two steps, three steps—They were passing him by; they were heading for Holloway—no, they were approaching Marshall. Jeremiah followed with stricken eyes the strides of the tall chief judge as he walked toward the owner of the handsome Shropshire.

There went the coveted blue ribbon. There went the little sack of cash money. The Almighty had forsaken him after all. And yet Jeremiah turned to Him in his agony. "Thy rod and Thy staff, they comfort me . . ."

"The judging committee of the Pike County Agricultural and Livestock Association hereby unanimously confers the blue ribbon and cash award upon Mr. Marshall's Shropshire Lad."

The crowd clapped and shouted. Marshall beamed and shook hands with the judges. Holloway scowled and kicked the dust with his toe. He took his lamb from the line, leading the other contestants from the arena. It seemed to Jeremiah that a cloud had covered the sun. He stood dazed and bewildered as Marshall came past with the blue ribbon proudly attached to his lamb.

"It's all right, Danny," Jerry whispered. "It's all right, boy."

Through unwanted tears Jeremiah saw the blurred figures beyond the rail. Tildy openly weeping, Granny dabbing at her eyes, while Uncle Hiram clamped savage teeth upon the butt of his cigar. But curiously enough the stranger was still smiling with bright, almost angelic calm. He remembered Granny's advice to come out walking proud like a Kincaid, and he straightened his narrow shoulders and began to lead his lamb from the ring. Already the crowd was turning away, unheedful, seeking some new amusement.

"Just a moment, folks," the leading judge shouted. "Wait a minute, young man."

Jeremiah paused uncertainly. "You mean me, sir?"

"I'm talking to you, son."

"I guess we can take our lickin'," Jerry said. "We lost fair and square."

"I like your spirit, boy," the judge said, "and I like your lamb. Only trouble is he's black. Sorta puts him in a class by himself."

The crowd laughed lazily as Jeremiah forced back the tears. He eyed the tall man before him suspiciously, half expecting ridicule; fearing even more any kindly words of consolation.

But the judge raised his hand for silence, and his stern, sincere voice awakened the smallest flame of hope in Jerry's mind.

"Wait, folks. I'm not trying to be funny. This lamb *is* in a class by himself. It happens sometimes that a crossbred lamb is born with almost perfect wool and conformation. Raised on a hill farm with no special breeding behind him, he shows what love and care can do in the production of livestock. He has good lines and a deep, fine fleece. No lamb has ever come into this ring better groomed than Kincaid's Dan Patch II. This young ram is a champion in every sense of the word, therefore . . ."

"Thou preparest a table before me in the presence of mine enemies . . ." said the voice in Jerry's mind.

"Therefore, we wish to confer on Mr. Kincaid and his lamb an award we have not made for the last three years—The Special Award of Merit."

Possibly the crowd was more kindly than Jeremiah had imagined, for they now broke all previous records in their noisy approval as the chief judge took a rosette and ribbon of royal purple silk from a small leather box.

Jeremiah had just reached the line in the Twenty-third Psalm which says very simply, "My cup runneth over."

From *So Dear to My Heart*
by Sterling North.

Exercise two. Listen to three radio programs that present different kinds of music—for example, rock and roll, jazz, opera, country and western, religious—and observe how the announcer for each uses the English language. What differences do you discover? Be ready to present your findings to your classmates in either spoken or written form.

Exercise three. In a television western, how does the language of the "good guys" differ from that of the "bad guys"? How does the language of the Indians differ from both? How does the language of the rancher or prospector differ from that of the person from the East? In what ways are these language differences important in the action of the drama?

Exercise four. Make a list of the technical words you use in a particular hobby or activity. Be prepared to explain them in class.

Exercise five. Visit your library and compare newspapers from various parts of the country to find examples of regional dialect. (Stories from the Associated Press or United Press are written for national wire services and will not reveal regional usages.) Study local advertisements, letters to the editor, and editorials. Take notes on your findings in order to report them to your classmates.

Exercise six. Reproduce an imagined conversation among members of your age-group. The setting might be a crowded table in a restaurant, the topic sports, school, or whatever timely subject comes to mind. Ask an older person to read this conversation and to mark any unfamiliar expressions. What does this exercise reveal about the young-old dimension of English?

CHAPTER TWO

Learning the Grammar of English

INTRODUCTION

We learn more about our native language in our first five years than in all the rest of our lives. In this chapter we first examine how preschool children learn the grammar of their language. They learn by listening to older people speaking around them, by imitating and practicing what they have heard, by playing with words, by using analogy, and by flashes of insight.

Next we consider what grammar children do actually learn. First, they learn the rhythm and music of English, one important part of their grammar. Then they learn words to go with the music, and how the words work in sentence patterns.

The signals of English grammar that help little children learn so much so fast about words and sentence patterns are of three main kinds: affixes, function words, and word order.[1] By these signals children can identify nouns, verbs, adjectives, and adverbs. Each of these parts of speech accepts typical affixes, combines with characteristic function words, and appears in its favorite positions in the basic sentence patterns. Because these signals are clear and regular, every normal child learns to recognize and use them at a very early age.

[1] *Affixes* are meaningful prefixes and suffixes. *Function words* are words like prepositions, determiners, conjunctions, and auxiliaries that show how nouns, verbs, adjectives, and adverbs work together in sentences. *Word order* is the arrangement of words in sentences.

HOW CHILDREN LEARN GRAMMAR

Dr. Ruth Hirsch Weir recorded the pre-sleep monologues of her two-and-a-half-year-old son, Anthony. When Anthony was put to bed at night and left alone, he always talked to himself before falling asleep. A microphone was placed on a chair near his bed and connected to a tape recorder outside his bedroom. Every night Anthony's parents started the tape recorder as soon as he began to speak to himself alone in the darkness. Between June and August 1961, Dr. Weir recorded nine tapes of her son's bedtime soliloquies, in which he practiced on English sentence patterns and drilled himself on English structures. Here are some snatches from Anthony's monologues—which sound like language laboratory exercises for learning English.

> "What color — What color blanket — What color mop — What color glass . . . Not the yellow blanket — The white. . . . It's not black — It's yellow . . . Not yellow — Red. . . . Put on a blanket — White blanket — And yellow blanket — Where's yellow blanket. . . . Yellow blanket — Yellow light. . . . There is the light — Where is the light — Here is the light."[2]

As Dr. Weir analyzed Anthony's sequences of words, she discovered three basic types: build-ups, break-downs, and completions. An example of a build-up is: "Sit down . . . Sit down on the blanket." An example of a break-down is: "Anthony jump down . . . Anthony jump." An example of a completion is: "And put it . . . Up there."

Anthony's favorite sentence type was the command: "Put on a blanket"; "Go buy some coffee"; "Don't jump." Then came declarative sentences like: "That's a boy"; "There is the light"; "Cobbers crossed the street." (Cobbers is his dog.) He also used question patterns like: "Where is Anthony's blanket?" "What's the matter?" "Where is the light?" Of course there were many mistakes that produced strange non-sentences. For instance, Anthony said: "What the take the blanket"; "Another other book please"; and "Bobo's going to sleeping." (Bobo is his toy.) Anthony used far fewer different words in his pre-sleep monologues than he did in his daytime speech.

Listening to slightly older children talking can reveal other interesting things about their language learning. For instance, three-year-old Billie was sitting at the breakfast table one morning, pretending that he was steering a car. His two hands were

---

[2] *Language in the Crib* (The Hague: Mouton & Co., 1962), p. 19.

clutching an imaginary wheel, which he was turning back and forth as though he were driving. Meanwhile he was making a noise like a car roaring down the road: "Rumm—rumm—rumm."

"Billie, are you driving your car?" his father asked him.

"No, Daddy," Billie replied, "I'm rumming."

This three-year-old child was inventing a new verb—*to rumm*—and he was using it properly, attaching the *-ing* suffix that it needed when he used it after "I'm."

In *The Five Clocks,* Dr. Martin Joos tells the story of a little girl named Lora and her language learning.[3] At fifteen months she could talk better than the average child of her age. Suddenly she stopped talking completely—even to herself when she was alone. That she still understood English was established one day when the family noticed that she was not wearing her glasses. Her brother explained the problem to her—that they would like her to find the glasses and put them on again—and she quickly led him to where she had left them a few hours before. There was nothing wrong with her intelligence or her understanding of English; she simply would not speak. Then one day when she was thirty-three months old she asked her brother as clearly and precisely as a five-year-old, "Shall I shut the door?" Apparently she had devoted those eighteen months of silence to

[3] (Bloomington: Indiana University Research Center in Anthropology, Folklore, and Linguistics, 1962), pp. 45-47.

intensive listening and had learned English properly. No baby talk for her! Dr. Joos believes that about one baby in a hundred clams up and learns his language in this way, chiefly by listening.

The nature of language often creates temporary difficulties and bafflement for young children. Here is a telephone conversation between four-year-old Lynn and her Aunt Margaret.

"Hello, Lynn. This is Aunt Margaret. How are you?"

"We watched TV today."

"That's nice, Lynn. How are you?"

"We watched TV today."

"I'm glad, Lynn. Is Billie there?"

"We watched TV today."

Lynn could not understand that the voice she heard on the telephone was her Aunt Margaret's, nor could she grasp the fact that she could communicate by language with someone she could not see. The other person and her language were unreal to her. Knowing that some spoken response was expected of her, she simply kept repeating the most important and real event of her day—that she had watched television. A few months later, Lynn grasped the idea that the voice she heard speaking on the telephone was really her aunt's, and that the words she heard were to be answered with other related words. Once she understood these facts she had taken a giant step forward in her comprehension of what language is. Kornei Chukovsky, the great Russian children's poet, tells about a five-year-old girl who asked her father, "Daddy, when I talked with you over the telephone, how did you manage to get into the receiver?" This little girl was one step closer than Lynn to understanding language.

Chukovsky also offers interesting observations on how children play with their language. A child often tries out new forms on a friendly adult—Betty-Detty, for instance, or Franky-Wanky. If the adult permits this word-play the child laughs merrily, because he has discovered that sometimes he can violate the language code and get away with it. In addition to delighting in a rhyming game, he is testing the flexibility of his language to find out how much it can stretch and bend without breaking. Here is an example from Chukovsky's book, *From Two to Five,* translated from Russian into English. Three-year-old Galia has invented a new game. She says:

"Mother, say 'clumsy'."

"Clumsy."

Galia rhymes: "Mumsie."

"Mother, say 'llama'."
"Llama."
Galia giggles and rhymes: "Mama."
"Mother, say 'salami'."
"Salami."
Galia roars with laughter: "Mommie."

And the game goes on and on.

These children, by experimenting, are learning the system of their language. All languages are organized systems, and learning the system is much more important than learning individual words. In fact, a child could not possibly learn every word separately and then learn how to combine them in all possible ways. He masters the system first and fits new learning into it.

Dr. Jean Berko has done some interesting research using nonsense words to prove and demonstrate how the child understands the system of his language.[4] She made up nonsense words and illustrated them with brightly colored pictures drawn on cards. Here is her picture of a wug, a birdlike cartoon character. She read the sentences on the card to each child, stopping at the blank space to let the child supply the proper form.

Dr. Berko found that preschool children using nonsense words could make plural nouns from singular nouns: *wugs;* progressive verb phrases like Billie's "I'm rumming": *He is zibbing;* and past tenses of verbs: *glinged, ricked, spowed, motted,* and

[4] "The Child's Learning of English Morphology," *Word,* XIV (1958), pp. 150-177.

bodded. First-grade children were much better at these language tasks than preschoolers, although both groups had trouble with adjectives. The first-graders were shown a picture of a dog with a few irregularly shaped green spots, another with a few more green spots, and a third with many green spots. The children were then told that the first dog had quirks on him, that the second dog had more quirks on him, and that the third dog had even more quirks on him. (*Quirk,* of course, was one of the nonsense words.) Then Dr. Berko said, pointing to each dog in turn:

"This dog is quirky.
"This dog is ________.
"And this dog is the ________."

She was trying, of course, to get the child to say that the second dog was *quirkier* and the last dog was the *quirkiest.* However, of the eighty children tested, only one supplied the correct forms. On the other hand, if she said, "This dog is quirky. This dog is quirkier. And this dog is the ________," omitting only the last form, about one-third of the children said *quirkiest.* They needed more of a hint; when she gave the comparative form, they were better able to supply the superlative form of the adjectives. These forms are not so common in English as are the regular plurals of nouns, the progressive verb phrases with *-ing,* and the regular past tenses of verbs.

Dr. Berko's research shows clearly that a child uses analogy in learning his language. That is, he observes the large groups of words he already knows, forms and applies generalizations about them, and on this basis is able to handle new words. An interesting contrast between child and adult language understandings was revealed through one of Dr. Berko's nonsense verbs—*gling.* The illustration of this verb showed a man exercising. The sentences with it said:

This is a man who knows how to gling.
He is glinging.
He did the same thing yesterday.
Yesterday he ________.

All the children tested said *glinged* to fill the blank. They based their choice on the analogy of most verbs in English, which form their past tense by adding *-ed.* However, when adults were tested with *gling,* some of them said *glang* or *glung,* irregular forms suggested by verbs like *ring* or *cling.* Only about ten of these kinds of irregular verbs exist in modern English: ring, sing, spring, cling, fling, sling, sting, string, swing, and wring. The young children had not heard the past tense forms of these verbs often enough to be awarc of the analogy which dictates the past tense of *gling.*

Exercise one. Test your power to use analogy on these other items which Dr. Berko asked her preschoolers and first graders. Be prepared to discuss generally the analogies you applied.

This is a man who knows how to spow. He is spowing. He did the same thing yesterday. What did he do yesterday? Yesterday he_____.

This is a wug.

This is a very tiny wug. What would you call a very tiny wug?

This wug lives in a house. What would you call a house that a wug lives in? (One little child answered this question with *wugwam.*)

This is a man who knows how to naz. He is nazzing. He does it every day. Every day he________.

This is a man who knows how to bing. He is binging. He did the same thing yesterday. What did he do yesterday? Yesterday he_____.

This is a man who knows how to zib. What is he doing? He is________.
What would you call a man whose job is to zib?

This is a niz who owns a hat. Whose hat is it? It is the__________hat.

Now there are two nizzes. They both own hats. Whose hats are they? They are the__________hats.

Although analogy is a powerful influence in language learning, it cannot completely explain how we come to know our language. It cannot explain, for example, how we learn that somehow all these word-groups are related.

1. They elected Bill captain.
2. Did they elect Bill captain?
3. When did they elect Bill captain?
4. Why did they elect Bill captain?
5. Where did they elect Bill captain?
6. They *did* elect Bill captain!
7. They did not elect Bill captain.
8. Bill was elected captain by them.
9. Their electing Bill captain . . .
10. Bill's being elected captain . . .
11. Bill's election as captain . . .
12. Bill, the captain, . . .

We know that all these word-groups are related because they all concern Bill and his captaincy. Yet they vary widely in their forms, word order, punctuation, and intonation—their rhythm and music. How do we learn that they are related?

Moreover, how do we learn to make new sentences, sentences that we have never heard before? Aside from formula sentences like "How are you?" or "I'll see you later," or "What time is it?" almost every sentence is a novel event. (A search through any piece of writing will only rarely turn up two identical sentences.) How do we learn to invent this constant flow of new sentences? And how do we learn to understand the flow of new sentences that other speakers of English create?

Statisticians have determined that if our learning depended on actually hearing, copying, and memorizing every possible sentence of twenty words in length we would need 100 years just to hear all the sentences once, at the rate of 3×10^{20} (300 billion billion) sentences per second. Even at this lightning rate we would have to remember each sentence perfectly after only one repetition. Nor would this pace allow time for sleeping, eating, or anything else. Then, even after we had heard all these twenty-word sentences, there would still be other sentences longer than twenty words. Obviously we do not learn our language in this way.

Perhaps, after all, learning our native language is an example of the creative process, the ability to relate previously unrelated things. Perhaps we have a built-in ability which enables us to pay attention to similarities and to ignore differences. Perhaps we must attribute the whole process to flashes of insight—those sudden "moments of truth" that we have all experienced. In an instant we grasp an idea completely and in terms of all our previous knowledge. We see exactly what it is and never forget it again. Perhaps all really important learning takes place in this way. Leo S. Vygotsky, a great Russian psychologist, explains the process as it may happen with children learning arithmetic:

> . . . the different steps in learning arithmetic may be of unequal value for mental development. It often happens that three or four steps in instruction add little to the child's understanding of arithmetic, and then, with the fifth step, something clicks; the child has grasped a general principle, and his developmental curve rises markedly.[5]

---

[5] From *Thought and Language* (Cambridge, Mass., The M.I.T. Press, 1962), p. 101.

LEARNING INTONATION

A college freshman used the three- and four-year-olds in her Sunday School class to prove that even very young children know the intonation patterns of English—that they react to the rhythm and music of the language even when they do not understand the words to the music. The teacher deliberately selected big words that the children did not yet have in their vocabularies, but used these words in familiar intonation patterns. For example, she said to three-year-old Bobby, "You don't want to be prosperous, do you?" She put strongest stress on *prosperous* and a disgusted fall in pitch at the end of the question. Bobby looked worried and answered emphatically, "Oh, no!" Then she asked, "You would like some disaster though, wouldn't you?" with strong stress on both *would*'s. Bobby clapped his hands and shouted, "Yes, yes, oh, yes!" Then she said in an intonation showing anger and disgust, "Bobby, you're a preposition!" Bobby looked anxious. When she added, "And you're a verb. Really you're almost an adverb," he burst into tears. To comfort him, she said with the intonation of consolation, "I was only teasing, Bobby, because you are really a noun and an adjective." Bobby felt better at once. Finding that all the children reacted in this same way, the college student succeeded in demonstrating that intonation patterns play a major role in communicating meaning.

Even before a child has words, we can tell by his intonation whether he is asking us a question or telling us something in statement form. Listen to a mother talking to her baby and observe how she responds to his intonation.

"Da, da?" the baby asks, his voice rising on the second *da.*

"Yes, dear," his mother replies, answering the question that her child has asked.

"Da, da," the baby says, his voice falling on the second *da.*

"You're welcome, darling," his mother replies, hearing the music of *Thank you* in her baby's intonation.

"Da, da, da, da," insists the child, pitching his babbling high to command attention.

"Take it easy," his mother tells him, "I'm coming as fast as I can."

Thus the baby comprehends and uses the rhythm and music of English before he has any words to go with the music.

PARTS OF SPEECH AND BASIC SENTENCE PATTERNS

In this part of this chapter we examine the signals that help children grasp the grammar of English. We examine the forms of words and how words work in sentences. The key words—nouns, verbs, adjectives, adverbs—are often called "parts of speech." They are important to children learning grammar because they have the clearest connection to the facts of experience. For example, notice how much meaning and emphasis the little boy in this story excerpt attaches to the word *cold.* He and his mother are outside on a dark fall evening. The mother tells the story.

> He pulled me toward the sandbox and I sat on the edge of it while he sent an exploratory finger into the cold and dirty sand.
>
> "Cold," he said, looking at me quizzically, "Cold."
>
> He came over and settled himself in my lap; I felt the cold from his cheeks in front of me in the dark. We sat for several minutes listening to bare tree branches rubbing against each other, watching the swaying shadows cast by the streetlight rocking in the wind and smelling the smell of cold earth. I shivered.
>
> "Cold," he squealed, putting his hands against my face, "Cold."
>
> He didn't protest when I picked him up and carried him toward the house.
>
> Once back in the warm envelope of the kitchen he slipped down and ran, jacket dangling half on, half off into the dining room corner where a begrimed elephant lay face down in the wheelbarrow.
>
> "Cold," he said, winding the elephant in an old hanky, "Cold."

From "Discovery"
by Pauline Hylkema.

NOUNS

Nouns are words like *boy, girl, book, butter, truth, grain, scissors,* and *sheep.* Probably you have learned this definition of a noun: "A noun names a person, place, thing, or idea." However, there are other quite definite ways of identifying nouns.

NOUNS are identified by certain suffixes. Suffixes are meaningful parts of words that can be attached to word stems to change the meaning of the stem. Here is a list of the most common suffixes that identify a word as a noun.

-age	coverage, wastage
-ance	deliverance, reliance
-ee	employee, appointee
-er	teacher, singer
-ment	encouragement, judgment
-ce	dependence, insolence
-cy	decency, privacy
-dom	kingdom, freedom
-ity	nobility, hospitality
-ness	goodness, sweetness
-ster	youngster, gangster
-ism	communism, republicanism
-ist	scientist, biologist
-ship	friendship, companionship
-hood	manhood, childhood

Exercise one.

1. Write three more nouns that use each of the following suffixes:

-ment -ity -ness -ist -hood

2. By adding typical noun suffixes produce nouns from these words:

read short appear old consistent

Another distinctive feature of nouns is their use of an *-s* or *-es* suffix in the written form. The majority of them form their plural by adding *-s* or *-es* to the singular. Examples are:

one robin	ten robins
my knee	both knees
every winter	several winters
that dish	those dishes

A few nouns still keep their Old English plural forms. Some of these are:

man	men
woman	women
child	children
ox	oxen

CERTAIN function words signal that a noun is coming up. These words are called *determiners.* The ones most often used are the definite and indefinite articles: *the, a, an.* Examples:

The camel with *the* low humps is enjoying *the* oasis.

He hunted all through *a* day that began with *a* shot at *an* elephant and ended with his bagging *an* antelope and *a* lion.

Another large group of determiners is the demonstratives: *this, that, these, those.* We will discuss these demonstratives used as pronouns later in this chapter. As determiners, they appear in positions like the following examples:

This girl sitting next to me likes *that* boy over there.

These elevators are handier than *those* stairs.

A third large group of determiners is the possessives: *my, our, your, his, her, its, their. His, her* and *its* can serve also as pronouns, which we will discuss later. As determiners, the possessives appear followed by the noun they signal. Examples:

My buddy expressed *his* disgust with *our* equipment.

I'll have to borrow *your* rope and *their* shovel.

A fourth large group of determiners is the cardinal numbers: *one* to *ninety-nine.* (*One hundred* begins over again by using *one* to signal that the noun *hundred* is coming up.) This entire group can serve also as pronouns. Examples:

One day he strolled in carrying *eleven* dahlias.

Four weeks ago the wind screamed for *seventy-two* hours without letup.

Among other determiners are:

all	some	few	several
any	more	either	every
both	no	neither	
much	each	most	

In the past you may have called these words "adjectives" because phrases like *every boy* resemble phrases like *big boy*, but in fact the phrases are different. As we will see when we discuss them, an adjective is a word that fits into both blanks in this test frame:[6]

The ________ noun seems very ________.
adjective *adjective*

We say *The big boy seems very big*, but we never say **The every boy seems very every*[7] or **The both boys seems very both.* We say *The dark night seems very dark* or *The soft butter seems very soft* but not **The each night seems very each* or **The much butter seems very much.* In other words, determiners are not adjectives.

Exercise two. In the following paragraph, pick out the determiners and the noun that each determiner signals.

> Yet the little creature lay snug like a kernel in the private ward of the Liverpool Central, with the door locked and a nurse giving her a blanket bath. Then in came tea, two meat sandwiches cut in triangles, a chocolate bun in a paper, a rice bun, a piece of plum cake and two slices of white bread and butter.
>
> From *National Velvet*
> by Enid Bagnold.

NOUNS also have certain favorite positions in English sentences: before and after verbs, and after prepositions. Prepositions are function words like *in, with, by, from,* and *around.* One way to recognize prepositions without having to memorize a list of them is to test them in this sentence.

The mouse ran ____________ the door.
preposition

Here is a list of prepositions that will test out in this sentence:

about	beneath	on
above	beside	opposite
across	beyond	over
after	by	round

[6] A test frame is a grammatical structure containing blank spaces into which words can be substituted to determine their part of speech.

[7] The star standing in front of a sentence means that a native speaker of English would not normally say this sentence.

against	down	through
along	for	to
around	from	toward
at	in	under
before	like	underneath
behind	near	up
below	off	with

A few prepositions do not fit this test sentence. They are:

among	during	regarding
but (meaning *except*)	except	since
concerning	of	until (or till)

Examples: We tiptoed *among* the tulips *of* Holland *until* (or *till*) sunrise. *During* this time we saw nothing *but* (or *except*) tulips. Later that day, the police talked to us *concerning* (or *regarding*) our adventure.

Exercise three. Read this paragraph and identify the prepositions. Then tell the noun they signal.

> I had a moment just then, I remember, of intense loneliness and fear. I was, I suspect, a trifle off my head like the rest of them by this time. I could hear nothing but the whistle and shudder of the storm. My eyes were blinded with snow, but behind the blindness was the reflection of the dancing lights. All London seemed to be leaping to get at me, and yet around and about me the wind was tearing to pull the city off its feet. In another moment perhaps it would succeed.
>
> From *Above the Dark Tumult*
> by Hugh Walpole.

Exercise four. On a sheet of paper write the prepositions that can fit into the blanks in this paragraph.

> I like coffee _______ the morning and _______ dinner, but not late _______ night. Then it keeps me _______ going to sleep. I prefer tea _______ coffee _______ the afternoon, especially _______ ice when the weather is hot. I take lemon _______ my tea, but the English take sugar and milk _______ theirs.

Another distinguishing feature of nouns is their relationship to pronouns. Pronouns substitute for nouns and noun phrases. For example, *he* can substitute for *Lincoln* in the sentence *Lincoln was president in 1862. Lincoln* refers to a definite person and is called a "proper noun." We could say, "He was president in 1862." The pronoun *he* can substitute also for noun phrases like these:

Determiner + noun:

The boy is here.
He is here.

Determiner + adjective + noun:

The big boy is here.
He is here.

Determiner + adjective + noun + prepositional phrase:

The big boy with the red hair is here.
He is here.

Personal Pronouns

The personal pronouns have powerful machinery for showing their possible positions in the sentence. Here are the forms of the personal pronouns.

Personal Pronouns: Singular

	Nominative	*Objective*	*Possessive*
1st person	I	me	mine
2nd person	you	you	yours
3rd person	he	him	his
	she	her	hers
	it	it	its

Personal Pronouns: Plural

	Nominative	*Objective*	*Possessive*
1st person	we	us	ours
2nd person	you	you	yours
3rd person	they	them	theirs

The first person refers to the speaker, the second person refers to the person spoken to, and the third person refers to the person or thing spoken about. Notice that each personal pronoun has singular and plural meanings even though the second person uses the same forms for both meanings. In each set of three, the first pronoun is the subject form, the second is the object form, and the third is the possessive form. Here are some examples of each use.

> *I* admired Miss Fletcher's poetry and *she* liked *mine* too. Mr. Baxter told *me* that *hers* was different in rhyme scheme from *his*, but *we* did not believe *him*. *They* thought *theirs* was similar to *ours*. Regarding poetry in general, Mr. Saxon pointed out that *it* is quite unlike prose. *It* has its own quality and prose has *its* too. Mr. Baxter had his opinion and Mr. Saxon had *his*.

Notice that in the last two sentences, *its* and *his* are used first as determiners signaling a noun coming up—*its own quality* and *his opinion*—and then as pronouns without a following noun—*its* and *his*.

Demonstrative Pronouns

Demonstrative pronouns are *this* and *that* in the singular, and *these* and *those* in the plural. Note that these are the same words that can be used as determiners, but they are pronouns when they are used without a following noun.

Demonstrative Determiners	**Demonstrative Pronouns**
I like *these* alligators.	I like *these*.
She marked *those* petunias.	She marked *those*.
He threw *this* javelin.	He threw *this*.
They watched *that* parade.	They watched *that*.

Many other words listed as determiners can serve also as pronouns. The way to tell the one from the other is that a determiner has a following noun phrase, whereas a pronoun has replaced a noun phrase.

Determiners	**Pronouns**
Have you *any* cheese?	No, I haven't *any*.
You can have *either* award.	He can have *either*, too.
I don't need *much* money.	I don't need *much*.
They have *few* enemies.	Yes, they have very *few*.
Each girl has an act to do.	*Each* will perform.

Exercise five. In the following sentences, identify and label all pronouns and determiners.

1. The bride was disappointed because she had only two bridesmaids when she had hoped for six.
2. Their negotiations with the kidnappers broke down completely because both sides lost patience with him.
3. Seahorses and goldfish are fun but I like turtles better than either.
4. Each February, those birds fly south but these stay in Connecticut.
5. Few neighbors want to spend every waking minute together, but probably all like some togetherness.
6. Her green thumb was one outstanding thing about her.
7. Jerry and his brother knocked at a door on the east side of the tavern several times.
8. Our little league team walloped yours yesterday.
9. Few objections can be raised by the judge about their responsibility or his.
10. It was so hot that neither cactus survived.

Exercise six. Here is a list of words that can be used as either pronouns or determiners. Write one sentence using each word as a determiner and one sentence using each word as a pronoun.

eight	both	that
much	some	seventy-six
either	its	
any	these	

Exercise seven. In the following paragraph identify the italicized words as nouns or pronouns and explain what clues you used to do so.

> *I* started to get up to go downstairs and eat, and then I saw *Davies. He* was sitting on the one *chair,* looking at the floor. Waking up from a *sleep* that had freshened *me* and put the *night's* business behind *me* some, I was surprised to see how bad he looked. His hair was tangled from running his *hands* through it, and he had a little white stubble of *beard.* He looked tired too, his face slack and really old, with big bruised *pouches* under the eyes. But *that* wasn't what made *him* look so bad. *It* was his forehead and eyes. His forehead was knotted and his eyes were too steady, like a careful *drunk's,* but not fogged in that way, but so bright *they* were mad. The *whites* of *them* were bloodshot too, and the rims a raw *red,* which made that light *blue* look even crazier.

From *The Ox-bow Incident*
by Walter Van Tilburg Clark.

Exercise eight. Write a four- or five-sentence paragraph in two versions, the first without pronouns. In the second version, substitute pronouns wherever it seems logical and effective to do so. Compare the two versions. What observations can you make about the relative clarity and effectiveness of the paragraphs?

VERBS

Verbs are words like *sprint, crouch, whack, take, bring,* and *become.* You probably have learned this definition of a verb: "A verb shows action, being, or state of being." While this definition is not untrue, it sometimes misleads us. There are more definite and reliable ways of identifying verbs.

VERBS are identified by certain prefixes and suffixes.

Prefixes:	en-	endear, engulf
	be-	bedevil, becloud
Suffixes:	-ate	hesitate, navigate
	-ize	socialize, agonize
	-ify	classify, clarify
	-ish	finish, furnish (This suffix can also mean *adjective:* the Span*ish* language, an Engl*ish* lesson; or *noun:* He speaks Span*ish* and Engl*ish.* We need other clues also.)
	-en	darken, lighten

Exercise one. Write three other verbs using each of the following suffixes.

-ate -ize -ify

IN ENGLISH all verbs use an *-s* to form their third-person singular present tense. All verbs use an *-ing* to form their present participle—the form found in such constructions as *He is walking.* All verbs have an infinitive form, which takes no ending and is often marked by *to:* He likes *to* walk. This *to* is not a preposition, since it is not followed by a noun. It functions as the marker of the infinitive, a verb form. Most verbs are "regular"; that is, they use *-ed* as a suffix to form the past tense, as in *He walked.* Regular verbs also use *-ed* to form the past participle. The past participle works with forms of *have:* He *has* walked. The following table shows these five different forms of five regular verbs.

Infinitive	*3rd Singular Present Tense*	*Past Tense*	*Past Participle*	*Present Participle*
(to) walk	walks	walked	walked	walking
(to) laugh	laughs	laughed	laughed	laughing
(to) change	changes	changed	changed	changing
(to) clean	cleans	cleaned	cleaned	cleaning
(to) play	plays	played	played	playing

The large majority of verbs follow this regular pattern of forms. The power of the pattern tends to pull the few irregular verbs into the regular pattern. When a new verb enters the language, it always follows the regular pattern. The few irregular verbs that still exist in English are very frequently used verbs. The child hears them so often that he eventually learns to use the irregular forms. Therefore they have stayed in the language. Here are some examples of these much-used irregular verbs.

Infinitive	*3rd Singular Present Tense*	*Past Tense*	*Past Participle*	*Present Participle*
(to) bring	brings	brought	brought	bringing
(to) buy	buys	bought	bought	buying
(to) think	thinks	thought	thought	thinking
(to) meet	meets	met	met	meeting
(to) sit	sits	sat	sat	sitting
(to) win	wins	won	won	winning
(to) stand	stands	stood	stood	standing
(to) find	finds	found	found	finding
(to) begin	begins	began	begun	beginning
(to) sing	sings	sang	sung	singing
(to) come	comes	came	come	coming
(to) run	runs	ran	run	running
(to) write	writes	wrote	written	writing
(to) speak	speaks	spoke	spoken	speaking
(to) take	takes	took	taken	taking
(to) know	knows	knew	known	knowing
(to) throw	throws	threw	thrown	throwing
(to) eat	eats	ate	eaten	eating
(to) give	gives	gave	given	giving
(to) see	sees	saw	seen	seeing
(to) do	does	did	done	doing
(to) go	goes	went	gone	going
(to) say	says	said	said	saying
(to) tell	tells	told	told	telling

Exercise two. The italicized verbs in these sentences are old-fashioned forms that are rarely if ever used in modern English as they appear here. Substitute the modern form in each case. What has happened to these verbs today? What is the powerful pattern underlying their changes?

1. Hidden in the broom closet, he *durst* not even clear his throat.
2. For three hours the defense attorney *pled* for the defendant.
3. Mrs. Guthrie has *baken* delicious Danish rolls for Flo's brunch.
4. The daring young man on the flying trapeze waved at the audience and *glode* through the air with the greatest of ease.
5. Alfred Newman *hove* the javelin 360 feet for a new world's record in the meet last Saturday.
6. The rooster has *crown* every day for the past week at twilight just as he *crew* this evening.

A THIRD distinctive feature of verbs is their use of auxiliaries. Auxiliaries signal that a verb is coming up, just as determiners signal a noun. English has three types of auxiliaries: modals, *be,* and *have.*

Modals are a small group: *must,* and the present/past pairs, *will/would, shall/should, can/could,* and *may/might.* They are always followed by the infinitive form of the verb without the infinitive marker *to.* Modals are peculiar in their lack of *-s* in the third-person singular present tense. That is, we say:

Bill will go   but not   *Bill wills go
Fran can play   but not   *Fran cans play
Joe must come   but not   *Joe musts come

The modals *will* and *shall,* as well as their informal contraction *'ll,* plus the unmarked infinitive are one way to express future time. For example:

Sam Hendricksen *will leave* for the Olympics next week.

They*'ll come* home on the tenth.

We can determine whether or not a word is a verb by inserting it in the test frame shown below. If it fits the space after a modal, it is a verb. (In the test frame, the words in parentheses may be inserted or left out as needed. Braces frame words of which one must be chosen.)

(The) noun { may / will / must / can } ______________ (the) (noun).
infinitive of verb

Choke, hurt, leave, be, and *bake* are verbs because they slip neatly into the blank after the modal:

The old chap will *choke.*

Nothing can *hurt* me.

Mr. McNulty must *leave* the country.

His name may *be* Peregrine Pickle.

You should *bake* the cake.

The second auxiliary that signals a verb is *have.* It is followed by the past participle form of the verb and usually refers to various kinds of past time. Examples:

The Connellys *had finished* the plan before they left the house.

The highwayman *has* just *entered* the inn.

Mrs. Bryan *has knocked* at the kitchen door every day this week.

The oranges *have ripened* early this year.

The electric eye *had triggered* the cameras.

These verb phrases are traditionally called "the perfect tenses."

If we find *have* occurring without a following past participle, it is not an auxiliary; it is the main verb of the sentence. Examples:

Ronnie *has* all the ice cream he can eat.

The Tigers *had* a chance for the pennant.

The buildings *have* cracks in their walls.

The football players always *have* steak before a game.

The third auxiliary is *be.* It is followed by the present participle, the verb form ending in *-ing.* Because *be* came from four different verbs centuries ago, it has a strange collection of forms. Each of the four verbs lost certain of its forms and the remainders joined. The present-day forms are:

Infinitive	*Present Tense*	*Past Tense*	*Past Participle*	*Present Participle*
be	am, are, is	was, were	been	being

Examples of the use of this auxiliary are:

The folks *are moving* west tomorrow.

Bob *was telling* strange stories to the children.

The candidates *will be working* on their speeches all night.

Dirk *has been calling* me "Georgie-Porgie" long enough.

Before she started to do her nails, she *had been debating* which color polish to choose, Moonlight Madness or Sunny Glad.

When *be* occurs without a present participle following, it is not an auxiliary; it is the main verb of the sentence. Examples:

John *is* a stinker.

The octopus *was* a monster.

Tommy's hands *were* always busy.

The silence *was* like a cool shadow.

The puddle *was* there all night.

This *is* the real world.

Often we find more than one auxiliary working with the verb:

They *have been* swimming all day.

We *might have* known that.

Bill *must have been* listening.

Exercise three. On a separate piece of paper list all the main verbs signaled by the italicized auxiliaries in the following sentences.

1. The policeman *was* waiting for Mr. Raye.
2. Swede *had* just bought a wristwatch.
3. Apple pies *were* baking in Mrs. Parker's oven.
4. He *must be* going to the rodeo.
5. Bertie *could* remember the thick soup.
6. The ocean beaches *will* be full today.
7. The ox *was* roasting on the hearth.
8. The second lady *must have been* working on the tent.
9. Four acrobats *were* balancing on the high wire.
10. Cora *could have* slammed the mailbox.

Exercise four. On a separate piece of paper list all the auxiliaries that signal the italicized main verbs.

1. The car was *thundering* down the road.
2. In the mornings Cora would *stand* in the door of the cabin.
3. The child had been *sneezing* for hours.
4. The wires must have been *hanging* loose all night.
5. She had fearfully *carried* the secret for one year.

6. The cameraman had *turned* his back on me.
7. They would have *been* happy to know the truth.
8. We could easily have *had* a new house last year.
9. A smart man will *be* careful.
10. They should have *arrived* before midnight.

Exercise five. On a separate piece of paper write an auxiliary to fill each space in the following sentences.

1. Outside it ______ beginning to snow.
2. The water ______ come through the tunnel.
3. The machines _____ _____ standing idle a long time.
4. Her whole life _____ _____ _____ passing through her mind.
5. The danger ______ be in any room.
6. In the powerhouse the turbines _____ _____ whirring steadily.
7. You _____ _____ expected a foolish answer from her.
8. Tina _____ _____ _____ standing beside Jim.
9. The storm _____ _____ _____ raging all night.
10. The kitchen utensils _____ _____ lying on the floor.

Exercise six. Pick out every form of *be* and *have* in the following paragraph from *The Old Man and the Boy* by Robert Ruark. In each case identify the form as a main verb or an auxiliary. Explain your reasons in each case. Are there any modal auxiliaries in the paragraph?

> This was as nice a smelling morning as I can remember. It smelled like it was going to work into a real fine-smelling day. The sun was up pretty high now and was beginning to warm the world. The dew was starting to dry, because the grass wasn't clear wet any more but just had little drops on top, like a kid with a runny nose. I sat on the stump for about a half-hour, and then I heard the dogs start, a mile or more down the swamp. Bell picked up the trail first, and she sounded as if church had opened for business. Then Blue came in behind her, loud as an organ, their two voices blending—fading sometimes, getting stronger, changing direction always.

A FOURTH distinctive feature of verbs is their power to classify English sentence patterns. In the next part of this chapter we will see how the three major types of English verbs produce five of the most familiar sentence patterns. These three major verb types are intransitive verbs, transitive verbs, and linking verbs. Intransitive verbs are those that appear in Basic Sentence

Pattern 1. Transitive verbs are those that appear in Basic Sentence Patterns 2 and 3. Linking verbs are those that appear in Basic Sentence Patterns 4 and 5. As you will see, the verb is the key to the various sentence patterns. Stripped down to its essential parts, an English sentence has two main divisions: (1) a noun phrase serving as subject, and (2) a verb phrase serving as predicate. It is the verb part that makes the difference, classifying the sentence into one or another of the basic sentence patterns.

VERBS AND SENTENCE PATTERNS

Basic Sentence Pattern 1

Noun Phrase/Subject + Intransitive Verb + (Adverb)

This pattern indicates that the sentence is composed of a noun phrase serving as subject, followed by an intransitive verb. The one important distinction of intransitive verbs is that they are not followed by a noun phrase. The parentheses around *Adverb* signal that it is optional. Any sentence may end with an adverb, either a single-word adverb or an adverbial phrase.

Examples of Basic Sentence Pattern 1:

His buddy laughed hysterically.

The corporal choked yesterday.

Our scout was squatting near the campfire.

Her grip tightened on the rifle.

The fingerprints matched exactly.

Exercise one. On a separate piece of paper write intransitive verbs to fill the blanks in these sentences of Basic Sentence Pattern 1. Use a different verb in each sentence. You may use single-word verbs or verb phrases containing auxiliaries. Examples:

Mary *wept* (or *must have been weeping,* or *was weeping*) desperately.

Three hours *have passed* (or *passed,* or *will pass*) quickly.

1. Tom ________ long after midnight.
2. Uncle Freeman ________ into the wall.
3. The knocking ________ after a while.
4. The machine ________ softly.
5. A seal ________ wildly.
6. The rapping ________ again.
7. The sun ________ brightly.
8. A trolley ________ past the store.
9. A door ________ silently.

Exercise two. Use each of these verbs in a sentence of Basic Sentence Pattern 1:

come	wave	twitch
swing	scowl	wander
bark	sing	laugh
speak		

Basic Sentence Pattern 2

Noun Phrase/Subject + Transitive Verb +
Noun Phrase/Direct Object + (Adverb)

Verbs are transitive when they permit a noun phrase serving as direct object to follow after them. The direct object noun phrase refers to something other than the noun phrase serving as subject.

Examples of Basic Sentence Pattern 2:

I can see the car clearly.
Jack is drawing the picture steadily.
You hid the bags under the snow.
The thing whacked me on the head.
Juanito held the revolver bravely.
The sun blistered the paint in the summer.

Many verbs are either transitive or intransitive depending solely on the presence or absence of the second noun phrase. For example, in *I can see the car, see* is transitive because of the noun phrase, *the car,* serving as direct object following *see.* On the other hand, in *I can see clearly, see* is intransitive because no noun phrase follows it. Only the adverb, *clearly,* appears. *Draw* is transitive in *Jack is drawing a cartoon,* but intransitive in *Jack is drawing steadily.*

Exercise three. On a separate piece of paper write transitive verbs to fill the blanks in these sentences of Basic Sentence Pattern 2. Use a different verb in each sentence. You may use single-word verbs or verb phrases containing auxiliaries. Examples:

The pilot *was gunning* (or *gunned,* or *will gun*) his engine.
Her sunburn *is hurting* (or *hurts,* or *must be hurting*) her.

1. Miss Mazie ________ pizza.
2. The town ________ taxes this year.
3. Albert ________ his outboard motor.
4. Squirrels ________ cats.
5. Douglas ________ them.
6. Mrs. McGuire ________ her lips.
7. The witch ________ her angrily.
8. Everybody ________ angleworms.
9. Lavinia ________ her hands.
10. Ken ________ his chickens.

11. Elmira ________ magic.
12. Shadows ________ the ravine.
13. Nobody ________ the police.
14. The moon ________ her hair.

Exercise four. Use each of these verbs in a sentence of Basic Sentence Pattern 2:

tear	manufacture	fold
capture	check	turn
design	close	hear
destroy		

Exercise five. Separate these sentences into those of Basic Sentence Pattern 1 and those of Basic Sentence Pattern 2.

1. They are studying algebra now.
2. Those people must have been fighting.
3. Sampson nodded his head wisely.
4. He wrote faithfully every day.
5. Grandfather was nodding by the fire.
6. The folks can write often.
7. The Filmores moved into the house in February.
8. Mathematicians study logically.
9. Melissa fought her sister constantly.
10. The tractor moved the house to Parkwood.
11. Mathematicians study logic.
12. Joe fought constantly.

Basic Sentence Pattern 3

Noun Phrase/Subject + Transitive Verb + Noun Phrase/ Indirect Object + Noun Phrase/Direct Object + (Adverb)

Transitive verbs in this pattern permit two noun phrases to follow them, each referring to a different thing and both different from the noun phrase serving as subject. The first noun phrase after the verb is the indirect object, and the second is the direct object. Two ways to identify the indirect object are (1) its position after the verb and before the direct object, and (2) its ability to move to the right of the direct object and stand after the prepositions *to* or *for.*

Examples of Basic Sentence Pattern 3:

The gang gave Joe a cake.

Mr. McNulty left Samantha the diamonds in his will.

Scrooge brought the Cratchits a goose at Christmas.

Daddy handed Sunny two letters.

The doctor sent us a message.

Sherlock Holmes told Dr. Watson the address.

Notice that if we move the indirect object to the right of the direct object after the prepositions *to* or *for*, the sentence's meaning does not change.

The gang gave a cake to Joe.

Scrooge brought a goose for the Cratchits at Christmas.

Exercise six. On a separate piece of paper fill the blanks in these sentences of Basic Sentence Pattern 3 with transitive verbs. Use a different verb in each sentence. You may use single-word verbs or verb phrases with auxiliaries. Example:

Bill *showed* (or *was showing,* or *will show*) me his coins.

1. Elizabeth ________ the children a story.
2. The manager ________ the winner a prize.
3. Dad ________ Raquel an envelope.
4. Jonah ________ Billy a song.
5. The policeman ________ me two tickets.

Exercise seven. In each of your sentences from the exercise above move the indirect object to the right of the direct object, inserting either *to* or *for* in front of the indirect object. Is the meaning essentially the same?

Basic Sentence Pattern 4

Noun Phrase/Subject + Linking Verb +
Noun Phrase/Predicate Noun + (Adverb)

The linking verb here makes the noun phrase that follows it refer to the same thing as the subject. The second noun phrase is a predicate noun. The two usual linking verbs that work in this pattern are *be* and *become,* but *stay* and *remain* are possible also.

Examples of Basic Sentence Pattern 4:

Egbert has become president suddenly.

His name is Rock Ransom in the movies.

The halfback became captain in September.
The cloud was a warning in the sky.
Elizabeth is an egotist without a doubt.
Hitler remained dictator for several years.
Malcolm stayed boss throughout the revolution.

Exercise eight. Divide these sentences into those of Basic Sentence Pattern 2 and those of Basic Sentence Pattern 4. Examples:

Basic Sentence Pattern 2: The pitcher hit a foul.
Basic Sentence Pattern 4: The pitcher is a ballplayer.

1. They dragged me down the stairs.
2. Radfield had his stenographer with him.
3. The attorney must have been Nils Svensen.
4. The senators heard snickering in the hall.
5. Advertising has the answer.
6. They remained stockholders in the company.
7. The jury convicted Briggs.
8. They elected directors for the campaign.
9. Dad could be a Democrat.
10. That muscle controls the thumb.
11. Dick has been a fighter.
12. Advertising is the answer.
13. The violinists had heard enough.
14. Dick had been fighting all challengers.

Exercise nine. On a separate piece of paper write nouns or noun phrases to fill the blanks in these sentences in order to produce sentences of Basic Sentence Pattern 4. Use a different noun or noun phrase in each sentence.

1. Letter writers must be ________.
2. Nurses become ________.
3. The people must have remained ________.
4. That song could be ________.
5. The victor stayed ________ for one year.
6. The yard became ________.
7. All men are ________.
8. Breathing is ________.
9. The earth became ________.
10. The graduates will be ________ tomorrow.

Basic Sentence Pattern 5

Noun Phrase/Subject + Linking Verb +
Adjective/Predicate Adjective + (Adverb)

The linking verb here is followed by a predicate adjective instead of a predicate noun. The predicate adjective refers to the noun phrase serving as subject. In this pattern, the linking verbs *taste, sound, feel, smell, look,* and *seem* work along with *be, become, stay,* and *remain.*

Examples of Basic Sentence Pattern 5:

The nurse was busy in the morning.
The mayonnaise tasted exotic on the pie.
Ellen was glassy-eyed with fatigue.
They remained calm throughout the hurricane.
My blister feels sore.

Exercise ten. Divide these sentences into those of Basic Sentence Pattern 4 and those of Basic Sentence Pattern 5. Examples:

Basic Sentence Pattern 4: Edward was a fool.

Basic Sentence Pattern 5: Edward was foolish.

1. Jenny was looking tired last night.
2. Johnson became President after the assassination.
3. His band was a success in Chicago.
4. The snow will be deep next winter.
5. Her arms felt thin that morning.
6. His father was mayor two years ago.
7. Our weather has stayed cool all summer.
8. Those sailors are dependable in an emergency.
9. That coffee smells wonderful after my nap.
10. The family may have felt stubborn about the tax.
11. The pigeons were a nuisance in the park.
12. My children sound happy on the playground.
13. The lemonade will taste delicious this afternoon.
14. Bullnose stayed a private for ten years.
15. Albert must have been honest in his opinion.

Exercise eleven. On a separate piece of paper write adjectives to fill the blanks in these sentences in order to produce sentences of Basic Sentence Pattern 5. Use a different adjective in each sentence.

1. My brain is feeling ________ this morning.
2. The pizza tastes ________.

3. All men become __________ sometime.
4. That dish will look __________ on the table.
5. The candidates seemed __________ after the election.
6. The candy smells __________.
7. The music sounded __________.
8. His skin remained __________ throughout the operation.
9. The policeman stayed __________ during the accident.
10. The team felt __________ because of the victory.

Reference Chart of
Five Basic Sentence Patterns

1. **Noun Phrase/Subject + Intransitive Verb + (Adverb)**
2. **Noun Phrase /Subject + Transitive Verb + Noun Phrase/Direct Object + (Adverb)**
3. **Noun Phrase /Subject + Transitive Verb + Noun Phrase/Indirect Object + Noun Phrase/Direct Object + (Adverb)**
4. **Noun Phrase/Subject + Linking Verb + Noun Phrase/ Predicate Noun + (Adverb)**
5. **Noun Phrase/Subject + Linking Verb + Adjective/ Predicate Adjective + (Adverb)**

Exercise twelve. Identify the basic sentence pattern of each of these sentences. Then explain how you recognized each pattern.

1. Mrs. Dietfelbinger found the Spragues a home.
2. Spike looked bleary-eyed.
3. Debris lined both tracks.
4. The platypus is safe in the cavern.
5. Bunker sagged under the news.
6. Snow immobilized the helicopters.
7. His home was his castle.
8. Franklyn taught Mrs. Cromper several languages.
9. Butch was dividing the volunteers into teams.
10. His attack failed miserably.

Exercise thirteen. In the following quotations state whether the italicized verbs are intransitive, transitive, or linking. Remember that the intransitive verbs have no following noun phrase serving as direct object. Transitive verbs have such a noun phrase. Linking verbs are followed either by a noun phrase serving as predicate noun or by an adjective serving as predicate adjective.

He *started* up the wooden rungs and I began climbing behind, up to the limb high over the bank. Phineas *ventured* a little way along it, holding a thin nearby branch for support. "*Come* out a little way," he said, "and then we'll *jump* side by side." The countryside *was* striking from here, a deep green sweep of playing fields and bordering shrubbery, with the school stadium white and miniature-looking across the river. From behind us the last long rays of light *played* across the campus, accenting every slight undulation of the land, emphasizing the separateness of each bush.

Holding firmly to the trunk, I *took* a step toward him, and then my knees *bent* and I *jounced* the limb. Finny, his balance gone, *swung* his head around to look at me for an instant with extreme interest, and then he *tumbled* sideways, *broke* through the little branches below and *hit* the bank with a sickening, unnatural thud. It *was* the first clumsy physical action I had ever seen him make. With unthinking sureness I *moved* out on the limb and jumped into the river, every trace of my fear of this forgotten.

From *A Separate Peace*
by John Knowles.

ONE interesting group of English verbs is called "two-word verbs." These are of two kinds. The first has a fixed, inseparable particle as its companion; the second has a movable, separable particle as its companion. For example, take *call on* and *call up.* We can say *Bill called up Mary,* and we can also say *Bill called Mary up.* We can say *Miss Fiditch called on Bill,* but we cannot say **Miss Fiditch called Bill on.* Here is a list of two-word verbs. Divide them into separable and inseparable types.

turn on	show off
look for	look like
put off	put away
shut down	take apart
run over	throw out

You probably have noticed that the words we are here calling "particles" are prepositions in other contexts. Here they are not prepositions because we pause after them, not before them, and because we pronounce them with too much emphasis. To understand these facts, contrast two uses of the word *over.* In the sentence, *I am looking over the new desk,* we can pause after *over* and put strong stress on it and the sentence means, "I am inspecting the new desk." Perhaps you are thinking of buying a new desk and you are looking it *over* to be sure you are getting your money's worth. Now if you pause before *over* and lighten the stress on it, the meaning changes to "I am peering over the top of the new desk." *Over* has become a preposition, and *the desk* is its object. Notice too that particles change the meaning of the verbs with which they work. For example, *look over* means "to examine" or "to inspect carefully." *Look* alone means "to view" or "to peer."

Exercise fourteen. On a piece of paper write two-word verbs that fit into the blanks in the following paragraph.

> Butch ______ early in the morning but did not want to ______. He wanted to ______ sleeping. He was ______ a bad cold and thought he should ______ his strength by ______. His mother, however, had ______ her mind not to let him ______ with staying in bed. She told Butch to ______ his clothes at once.

Exercise fifteen. In these sentences using two-word verbs, identify sentences of Basic Sentence Pattern 1 and Basic Sentence Pattern 2 by recognizing the difference between particles and prepositions. Examples:

> *Basic Sentence Pattern 1:* He went over the bridge. ("He crossed the bridge." An intransitive verb followed by a prepositional phrase.)
>
> *Basic Sentence Pattern 2:* He went over the lesson. ("He reviewed the lesson." *Went over* is a two-word verb; *the lesson* is its direct object.)

1. The car could turn on a dime.
2. The company will turn on the electricity tomorrow.
3. The children ran across the street.
4. The auditor ran across an error in the records.
5. The invalid looked out the window.
6. Foam put out the fire.
7. The driver turned off the road.
8. The plumber turned off the water.
9. The messenger called up the speaking tube to Smith's apartment.
10. Bill called up his wife.

Exercise sixteen. Here is an amusing discussion on particles, prepositions, and two-word verbs. You will probably be surprised to realize that we have so many uses for *up*.

"What's *up*?" asks Joe College. And for once he's not spoiling for a lark, but puckering his puzzled brow over a problem in parsing. It may have been "Come out from up in under there" or something even trickier. It is better, of course, to avoid such syntactical pitfalls, but if the problem comes up, we are bound to face up to it. We can give him an answer which will bear up, hold up, or stand up under a later and more intensive scrutiny; or we can give one sufficiently dogmatic, erudite, or ambiguous to quiet him (i.e., shut him up). Better yet, we can tell him to study up on his parts of speech and look up the words in his dictionary, and we can promise to take it up at the next class meeting.

Joe may get little help outside, however, for handbooks rarely treat *up* adequately and many unjustly malign this most versatile word in the English language. One glossary of faulty diction declares: "Don't say clean up my room; say clean my room." Another says: "*Faulty.* I must finish up the work. *Better.* I must finish the work." . . .

As an intensive, *up* is often attached to a verb to give added emphasis or vigor. It imparts a feeling of completeness, finality, or finish—something beyond or above the usual performance. It is like the last flick of the dustcloth in cleaning up a room or the completion of the last detail in finishing up the work. Its use may be compared to that of the intensive as distinguished from the reciprocal use of reflexive pronouns: She herself is to blame, and she herself must suffer the consequences. Nothing is added by the reflexive except emphasis.

The colloquial expressions illustrating the intensive use of *up* are more interesting than more formal ones, though this use can be as easily illustrated from formal or literary language. "Clean up your feet and don't dirty up my rug!" is informal but intensive in both its positive and preventive aspects. During times of particular stress and strain . . . students find *up* . . . an invaluable aid to intensive effort. They "cram up," "bone up," "study up," "book up," take "make-up exams," and try to "catch up". . . . "Mopping up" is a military term thoroughly established during World War II and suggests the vigor, finish, and finality so often associated with *up*. The "souped up" jalopy came in with the "hot-rodders." The "pin-up" girl, we suppose, is someone's idea of the feminine *ne plus ultra*.

The intensive vigor and the versatility of *up* is nowhere better demonstrated than in the ease with which it has often supplanted *down*—where the latter would be more exact or logical: We slip up and go down. We usually sit down when we sit up or stay up to study. We slow up when we slow down. We are often down when we are laid up with rheumatism or a bad cold. Only the old-timers "put down" fruit for the cellar before our little furry friends dig down to hole up for the winter. If the bad men who start out to shoot up the town really finish up the job, it is likely to be all up with those who are down. We drink up or eat up what is good—down, only when it's bad. When a man starts down, we are likely to say: He's about "used up," "washed up," "finished up," or "done up"; or he's ready to "fold up" or "throw up the whole business." He may have "cracked up," "been all broken up," or been ready to "give up." And when he's completely down, it's "all up" with him. Best advice on such occasions, we are told: "Cheer up," "brace up," "buck up," or "perk up," old man! You can't get any further down. The writer once had a rough time with a recalcitrant cow that wouldn't give up and give down her milk. Her name was Upsy Daisy. I'm getting a little mixed up now. If you're not already convinced, drop up and see me sometime.

Another frequent function of *up* may be called that of a semantic adjunct. It extends, modifies, or completely changes the meaning of the word to which it is attached. We can make up a list, the bed, a batch of cookies, a foursome, lost time, or our faces. We can make up after a lovers' quarrel or, less properly, we can try to make up to (please or impress) the boss—or the boss's daughter.

Often the meaning is completely changed by *up*. I was too near finished up to finish the work. She was mixed up when she mixed that stuff. Blot your theme papers before you blot them up. He'd rather show me up than show me. The employee fired up (cf. flared up, talked up, spoke up) in front of the boss, and the boss ups and fires him. We may be blown by the wind (or the lack of it); or we may be blown up by self-adulation or an atomic bomb—with an extra *up* added for hydrogen. Junior is a good boy when he acts like his mother; a bad boy when he acts up like his father. We may clean the city with a fire hose; to clean it up may involve a crusade against dirty politics and end up in a shake-up. "To wait for him" often suggests faith and tenderness; "to wait up for him" reminds us of Tam's wife, "nursing her wrath to keep it warm."

When the addition of *up* changes the meaning of the word to which it is attached, we may often find it convenient to explain the combination in terms of one-word equivalents. Chameleonlike the combinations take color or meaning from their surroundings or context: She swept up the aisle. Was she dressed in shimmering silks and satins or equipped with broom and pan? She was held up in Chicago. The phrase is meaningless without context: She was held up (robbed) by an armed bandit. She was held up (delayed) for an hour by a grounded plane.

From "What's Up"
by Howard E. Packenham.

Exercise seventeen. Write an essay on *down* similar to the one on *up*. It is possible to use almost as many *down's* as *up's*.

Exercise eighteen. Here is a set of sentences using all the Basic Sentence Patterns. Identify each by its number.

1. Factories were hiring all comers during World War II.
2. Carter lost his incentive that night.
3. The Apaches galloped into the corral.
4. Skiing had been his hobby for years.
5. His office will be dusty after the tornado.
6. His mother left him a house.
7. Carney ran away from home at nineteen.
8. He gave up his job yesterday.
9. The auctioneer was discreet with his hammer.
10. His health collapsed during the winter.
11. He made up his mind later.
12. The champion could have come back into the fight.
13. The waiter is serving Jeffrey breakfast.
14. A shotgun went off suddenly.
15. The world was his oyster.

ADJECTIVES

Adjectives are words like *big, pretty, beautiful, tall.*

ONE excellent way to identify adjectives is this test frame:

The ________ noun(s) seem(s) very ________.
adjective *adjective*

Examples:

The *red* shoe seems very *red.*

The *bright* stars seem very *bright.*

This test frame shows the two favorite positions of adjectives in English sentences. One is between a determiner and its noun, and the other is in the predicate serving as predicate adjective after a linking verb. The word must slip smoothly into *both* positions to be an adjective, since many nouns and verbs will work in the first position but not in the second. The reason is that *very* is an unusual kind of adverb, which works only with adjectives and adverbs. Thus it filters out nouns and verbs from the adjective class. For instance, we reject this sentence:

*The *baby* doll seems very *baby.*
noun

Baby is a noun; it will fit into the first position but not into the second. We can call *baby* a noun-modifier because it modifies *doll,* the noun headword. A headword is a noun, verb, adjective, or adverb expanded to a phrase by other words, called its modifiers. For example:

the tall man outside in the convertible

> *Man* is the noun headword modified by *the, tall, outside, in the convertible.*

must always work hard until midnight

> *Work* is the verb headword modified by *must, always, hard, until midnight.*

very quick with his answer

> *Quick* is the adjective headword modified by *very* and *with his answer.*

too soon after the war

Soon is the adverb headword modified by *too* and *after the war.*

We reject this sentence too:

*The *living* doll seems very *living.*
present participle of verb

Living is a verb; it fits neatly into the first position but not into the second. We can call *living* a noun-modifier because it modifies *doll,* the noun headword.

Exercise one. Here is a list of words to be tested in the adjective test frame. The word must be used in exactly the form given, and it must fit smoothly in both positions to be a true adjective.

1. newspaper	*6.* dancing
2. Baltimore	*7.* promised
3. modern	*8.* old
4. full	*9.* calypso
5. two	*10.* interesting

Exercise two. Here are sets of three noun phrases. Test them in the adjective frame to identify the adjectives. Example:

arid desert Sahara desert irrigated desert

The *arid* desert seems very *arid. Arid* is an adjective because it fits both blanks.

*The *Sahara* desert seems very *Sahara. Sahara* is not an adjective because it fits only the first blank. It is a noun.

*The *irrigated* desert seems very *irrigated. Irrigated* is not an adjective because it fits only the first blank. It is a verb.

1. Red Cross nurse	registered nurse	cheerful nurse
2. swinging door	old door	house door
3. interesting story	revised story	feature story
4. delicious dinner	TV dinner	boiled dinner
5. school marks	high marks	identifying marks
6. tanned leather	shoe leather	soft leather
7. rose bush	beautiful bush	flowering bush
8. bright boy	developing boy	messenger boy
9. dress shirt	white shirt	ironed shirt
10. maple tree	growing tree	tall tree
11. condemned building	old building	office building
12. red top	spinning top	bottle top

ADJECTIVES are identified by certain suffixes.

-y	funny, crazy
-ive	responsive, cooperative
-able	comfortable, agreeable
-ful	delightful, cheerful
-less	thoughtless, reckless
-ar	regular, circular
-ary	honorary, customary
-ic	poetic, comic
-ish	slavish, childish
	(This suffix can also mean *verb* [as in fin*ish* and van*ish*] or *noun* [as in He speaks Engl*ish*]. We need other clues also.)
-ous	dangerous, fabulous
-ent	different, intelligent
-en	woolen, wooden
-ed	beloved, aged
-ing	fascinating, interesting

Exercise three. Make two other adjectives using these suffixes.

-ish -able -ful

ANOTHER distinctive feature of adjectives is that many form their comparative by adding *-er* and their superlative by adding *-est* to their positive form. Dr. Berko compared her *quirky* dog to a *quirkier* dog and then to the *quirkiest* dog of all. Examples:

Positive	*Comparative*	*Superlative*
long	longer	longest
great	greater	greatest
cold	colder	coldest
funny	funnier	funniest

Adjectives having three or more syllables form their comparatives and superlatives by using *more* and *most* instead of *-er* and *-est.* Examples:

Positive	*Comparative*	*Superlative*
enthusiastic	more enthusiastic	most enthusiastic
fascinating	more fascinating	most fascinating
wonderful	more wonderful	most wonderful
favorable	more favorable	most favorable

Although the ability to use *-er* and *-est* is a distinctive feature of adjectives, a very few adverbs also can be compared by these suffixes. Example:

He drove fast. His brother drove faster. James drove fastest.

Exercise four. Use the comparative of these adjectives in interesting sentences.

1. brilliant
2. gray
3. particular
4. clean
5. busy
6. sunny
7. friendly
8. typical
9. famous
10. wild

Exercise five. Pick out the adjectives in this passage and explain how you recognize them as adjectives.

It was a woman, all alone in the bitter night. She was a tall woman with gray hair and a handsome face. She wore a coat that would have been suitable for an evening at the opera. It had a bit of fur about it but no warmth. Her dress was thin and her scarf was quite inadequate.

She loomed out of the darkness like a demented queen from some Shakespearean play. Why she was alone we never knew. When she saw us she hesitated, and if we had been Russian soldiers, I am sure she would have jumped into the canal and tried to escape, but when she heard us speaking English she came up to us through the icy air and spoke rapidly in French. "I have been walking three days," she said. "Before that the Russians caught some of us and held us in a bunker for forty-eight hours. Some of us were shot. I escaped. How far must I go now?"

"Only one more kilometer to the hut," McGurn lied to encourage her.

"I can make that. If I have survived the last three years, I can survive the last kilometer."

Then she went into the cold mists. Who was she? We never knew. What torments was she fleeing? We could only guess. But as she went down the silent canal, a great gaunt figure of triumphant tragedy, fighting against the darkness totally alone, I saw something that haunts me still. She wore high-heeled shoes and had worn them through the long miles, the Russian prison and the swamps.

From *The Bridge at Andau*
by James A. Michener.

ADVERBS

Adverbs are words like *quickly, rapidly, here, somewhere, soon,* and *then.*

ADVERB sentence position is the most useful clue in identifying them. This test frame shows their favorite position.

The noun verbs the noun ________.
adverb

Examples:

The photographers clicked their shutters *frantically.*

The auctioneer accepted the bid *immediately.*

I met Jim *yesterday.*

Although the final position is the one we can best use for identifying them in the test frame, adverbs can appear in other positions in the sentence too. Examples:

The photographers *frantically* clicked their shutters.

Frantically the photographers clicked their shutters.

The auctioneer *immediately* accepted the bid.

Immediately the auctioneer accepted the bid.

Yesterday I met Jim.

Several adverbs can occur together in a sentence, of course. When they do, they follow fairly strict rules of word order. When both place and time adverbs occur, place precedes time.

He played *upstairs yesterday.*
Place *Time*

Adverbs of manner are the most movable of adverbs. They can occur after the object and before adverbs of place and time.

She was singing a song *quietly upstairs yesterday.*
Manner *Place* *Time*

Adverbs of manner can occur also before the subject as in:

Gradually, Frank moved the tractor away from the precipice.

They can occur also between the subject and the verb, as in:

Frank *gradually* moved the tractor away from the precipice.

Or they can occur between the adverbs of place and time, as in:

She was singing upstairs *quietly* yesterday.

Never, however, can they occur between the verb and its object, as in:

*Frank moved *gradually* the tractor away from the precipice.

A non-sentence like this would be uttered by a foreigner, not a native speaker of English.

Adverbs are not always movable. Sometimes they are an essential part of the predicate. In such cases, moving them destroys or distorts the meaning of the sentence. For example, in:

The children will be going *inside*.

the adverb *inside* is not movable because it is an essential part of the predicate. Moving *inside* to front position produces an ambiguous sentence:

Inside the children will be going.

Moving *inside* to middle position changes the meaning of the sentence.

The children *inside* will be going.

The movability of adverbs depends on the meaning we wish to communicate.

Exercise one. Insert the adverbs listed at the left into all possible positions in the sentence to their right. For example, in the sentence:

Mr. Bigdome sabotaged Tremblechin's suggestion.

we can insert the adverb *tacitly* into the three adverb positions:

Tacitly, Mr. Bigdome sabotaged Tremblechin's suggestion.

Mr. Bigdome *tacitly* sabotaged Tremblechin's suggestion.

Mr. Bigdome sabotaged Tremblechin's suggestion *tacitly*.

1. soon—I had my fill of plain living and high thinking.
2. reluctantly—All the girls wore something red.
3. yesterday—Ellen and I were standing on chairs cheering.
4. probably—Mama will make a great fuss over her bank account.
5. home—They came home at three A.M.
6. now—They are having a battle royal in Hoboken.
7. outside—A huge portico surrounded the mansion.
8. sweetly—The alligator devoured the bondsman.
9. frankly—Allbright admired that big, raw-boned girl.

MOST adverbs can be classified into three large types: manner, place, and time. Manner adverbs are sometimes called "thus-type" adverbs, since *somehow* can be substituted for them. They answer the question *How?* (and *How much? How far? How long? How often?*). They are most often made from adjectives plus the *-ly* suffix. Examples in the exercise sentences above are *tacitly, reluctantly, sweetly, frankly,* and *probably.*

Place adverbs are sometimes called "there-type" adverbs, since *someplace* can be substituted for them. They answer the question *Where?* Examples in the exercise sentences above are *home* and *outside.*

The third large type are adverbs of time, often called "then-type" adverbs. *Sometime* can be substituted for them, and they answer the question *When?* Examples in the exercise sentences above are *yesterday, now,* and *soon.*

A few adverbs operate with adjectives and adverbs only, not with verbs as adverbs of manner, place, and time do. These unusual adverbs are sometimes called *qualifiers* or *intensifiers.* Here are some of them:

It was a *very* strange molecule.
He coddled his *rather* low-priced convertible on curves.
Somewhat surprisingly, he failed to show up for final exams.
His *really* intelligent daughter, Virginia, was born on the ranch.
Roundtree studied in a *quite* delapidated library.
Ronald teased Lizbeth not wisely but *too* well.
Rembrant roasted chestnuts *more* often than marshmallows.
Beach's election was protested *most* violently by the board.
He fled up the circular staircase *pretty* quickly.

ONE prefix and a few suffixes are characteristic of adverbs.

Prefix:	a-	ahead, away
Suffixes:	-ly	quickly, sweetly
	-ward(s)	backward, backwards
	-where	somewhere, elsewhere
	-wise	likewise, cornerwise

Notice that the most common suffix, *-ly,* can also mean adjective when it is added to nouns, as in *friendly* and *homely.* The *-ly* that means adverb is added to adjectives.

Exercise two. Write other adverbs using the suffixes *-ly* and *-wise.*

Exercise three. Explain how the italicized adverbs in the following paragraphs can be identified as adverbs.

> The fine knife came *out* again and was whetted *again* just as *carefully* as it had been the first time. Jody held the pony's head *up* and the throat taut, while Billy felt up and *down* for the right place. Jody sobbed once as the bright knife disappeared into the throat. The pony plunged *weakly* away and then stood still, trembling *violently*. The blood ran *thickly* out and up the knife point and cross Billy's hand and into his shirtsleeve.
>
> From *The Red Pony*
> by John Steinbeck.

> So in spite of her protests, I left Liddy *alone* and went *back* to the east wing. *Perhaps* I went a little *faster* past the yawning blackness of the circular staircase; and I could hear Halsey creaking *cautiously* down the main staircase. The rapping, or pounding, had ceased, and the silence was *almost* painful. And then *suddenly*, from *apparently* under my very feet, there rose a woman's scream, a cry of terror that broke *off* as *suddenly* as it came. I stood frozen and still. Every drop of blood in my body seemed to leave the surface and gather around my heart. In the dead silence that followed it throbbed as if it would burst. More dead than alive, I stumbled into Louise's bedroom. She was not *there!*
>
> From *The Circular Staircase*
> by Mary Roberts Rinehart.

Summary Exercises

Exercise one. In the following sentences, word order, affixes, and function words signal parts of speech. Pick out the nouns, verbs, adjectives, and adverbs, and explain orally how you recognized them.

1. Two rather yody makons blopped.
2. Some franctious backpinders glang a sangly flimflam.
3. An orbuly basseled the ragroes.
4. The new, damorphic framograph was suppulsing behind a rense.
5. Those nankisms are glanter ronglers.
6. Around their froncy there is a snawlish stortee blunking her macroperology.

Exercise two. Use each of the following words in two sentences to show that it can be both a noun and a verb. In the first sentence use it as a noun; in the second sentence, as a verb.

market	snow	touch
cloud	sail	horse
run	hit	blanket
field		

Exercise three. Here is a set of sentences in which certain words are italicized. On a separate piece of paper list all the possible parts of speech that each word could be. Then underline which one it is in the given sentence.[8] Example:

His excessive *speed* led to a serious accident. Verb, noun.

1. The torrential rains began on *schedule.*
2. Drive *fast.*
3. The folks like to *play* anagrams.
4. A *pretty* old salesgirl sold me the hat.
5. The city *fathers* are in uneasy conclave tonight.
6. Dave often *clubs* his conscience into obedience.
7. Miss Stroh is my *German* friend.
8. Don't *mind* me, girls; I'm just a two-star general.
9. *Quiet* music calms savages.
10. These *tours* are famous for frustrating the tourists.
11. Abe had the same sprightly *waddle* as his father.
12. Please *hand* me the screwdriver.
13. The sharp *pain* was beginning to ease.
14. The *relative* humidity is 98%.
15. Let's *face* it now.

Exercise four. We know that adverbs like *very,* which work with adjectives and adverbs but not with verbs, can signal either an adjective or an adverb coming up. Each of these sentences contains one of these adverbs. State whether it is used with an adjective or an adverb.

1. The corned beef tasted *very* delicious.
2. Will had a *somewhat* overwhelming stamp collection.
3. Mr. Jenkins was *quite* worried about his season tickets.
4. She's my wife even though she is *very* clearly your sister, too.
5. Mary Belle is *too* young to tango.
6. The butler signed the check *most* expeditiously.
7. Bowser's protective value is *pretty* low.
8. Her folks are *more* friendly than his.
9. Alan was a *rather* young executive to have ulcers.

---

[8] This exercise was suggested by Problem One, pp. 37-38 in John C. Mellon's *The Grammar of English Sentences* (Culver, Indiana: Culver Military Academy, 1964).

Exercise five. Test the italicized words in these sentences in test frames and by the suffixes they may use, and list what part of speech each one is.

1. The *stone* wall is gray.
2. The *gray* wall is stone.
3. *Stonewall* Jackson was a general.
4. They fought a *hockey* contest.
5. They fought a *decisive* contest.
6. They fought a *tight* contest.
7. They played the *deciding* match.
8. They admired the *rolling* table.
9. They admired the *coffee* table.
10. They admired the *blond* table.
11. The bell sounded *sweet.*
12. The bell sounded *sweetly.*

Exercise six. Make nouns from the verbs and adjectives listed below by adding suitable noun suffixes.

supplicate	soft	social
propose	magnificent	active
infer	indulgent	short
confide		

Make verbs from the nouns and adjectives listed below by adding suitable verb suffixes or prefixes.

courage	bright
horror	beauty
quick	magnet
tender	mad

Make adjectives from the nouns and verbs listed below by adding suitable adjective suffixes.

magnet	indulge	slave
impress	courage	endure
recognize	breath	portent
danger		

Make adverbs from the adjectives and nouns listed below by adding suitable adverb prefixes and suffixes.

desperate	front	long
quick	insistent	indulgent
side	different	magnificent
central		

Exercise seven. In each of these paragraphs identify two different examples of nouns, verbs, adjectives, adverbs, determiners, auxiliaries, and prepositional phrases and explain how you recognized them. In the case of verbs, state also whether the form is the infinitive, the present tense, the past tense, the past participle, or the present participle.

> Two nights before the Derby, she was at a big party in town, when one of her rushes of anxiety about her boy, her first-born, gripped her heart till she could hardly speak. She fought with the feeling, might and main, for she believed in common sense. But it was too strong. She had to leave the dance and go downstairs to telephone to the country.
>
> From "The Rocking Horse Winner"
> by D. H. Lawrence.

> The train left the station in Marseilles and there was not only the switch-yards and the factory smoke but, looking back, the town of Marseilles and the harbor with stone hills behind it and the last of the sun on the water. As it was getting dark the train passed a farmhouse burning in a field. Motor cars were stopped along the road and bedding and things from inside the farmhouse were spread in the field. Many people were watching the house burn. After it was dark the train was in Avignon. People got on and off. At the newsstand Frenchmen, returning to Paris, bought that day's French papers.
>
> From "A Canary for One"
> by Ernest Hemingway.

> "And this is how I see the East. I have seen its secret places and have looked into its very soul; but I see it always from a small boat, a high outline of mountains, blue and afar in the morning; like faint mist at noon; a jagged wall of purple at sunset. I have the feel of the oar in my hand, the vision of a scorching blue sea in my eyes. And I see a bay, a wide bay, smooth as glass and polished like ice, shimmering in the dark. A red light burns far off upon the gloom of the land, and the night is soft and warm. We drag at the oars with aching arms, and suddenly a puff of wind, a puff faint and tepid and laden with strange odors of blossoms, of aromatic wood, comes out of the still night—the first sigh of the East on my face. That I can never forget. It was impalpable and enslaving, like a charm, like a whispered promise of mysterious delight."
>
> From "Youth"
> by Joseph Conrad.

Exercise eight. Here are four short poems, all of which use the same device to create humor. Analyze the poems to discover the device. Then rewrite the poems in prose showing the authors' meanings. The first poem is by David McCord from *Odds Without Ends;* the last three, by Felicia Lamport, are from *Scrap Irony.*

Gloss

I know a little man both ept and ert.
An intro-? extro-? No, he's just a vert.
Sheveled and couth and kempt, pecunious, ane,
His image trudes upon the ceptive brain.

When life turns sipid and the mind is traught,
The spirit soars as I would sist it ought.
Chalantly then, like any gainly goof,
My digent self is sertive, choate, loof.

Hint

There never is trouble in finding a spouse
For the ebriated man with the lapidated house.

Cretion

Dora, a daisical damosel,
Was lively and gainly and ert.
She should have done well,
But the hapless girl fell
For a feeble, fatigable squirt
Named Bert.

Astrous Ending

When he clutched his solar plexus
His necrology seemed mote,
But they found his illness fectious
And they cured it with a dote.

Fine Old Professor

The students who had gnored him
Universally adored him
And he died beknownst and famous:
a gnominious gnoramus.

Exercise nine. Here is Lewis Carroll's famous "Jabberwocky" poem from *Through the Looking-Glass.* Read the poem. In it, many of the nouns, verbs, adjectives, and adverbs—the parts of speech—are nonsense words invented by Carroll. However, prepositions (like *in, by, through, with*), conjunctions (like *and* and *so*), determiners (like *the*) are real English words. These are function words; that is, they have the function of showing relationships among the parts of speech.

Jabberwocky

'Twas brillig, and the slithy toves
  Did gyre and gimble in the wabe:
All mimsy were the borogoves,
  And the mome raths outgrabe.

"Beware the Jabberwock, my son! 5
  The jaws that bite, the claws that catch!
Beware the Jubjub bird, and shun
  The frumious Bandersnatch!"

He took his vorpal sword in hand:
  Long time the manxome foe he sought— 10
So rested he by the Tumtum tree,
  And stood awhile in thought.

And, as in uffish thought he stood,
  The Jabberwock, with eyes of flame,
Came whiffling through the tulgey wood, 15
  And burbled as it came!

One, two! One, two! And through and through
  The vorpal blade went snicker-snack!
He left it dead, and with its head
  He went galumphing back. 20

"And hast thou slain the Jabberwock?
  Come to my arms, my beamish boy!
O frabjous day! Callooh! Callay!"
  He chortled in his joy.

'Twas brillig, and the slithy toves 25
  Did gyre and gimble in the wabe:
All mimsy were the borogoves,
  And the mome raths outgrabe.

Substitute for each nonsense word a real English word of the same part of speech and with the same number of syllables. Be sure that your translation of the poem makes sense. Be sure also that once you have decided on a substitute for a word that you always use that same English word for that particular nonsense word. In doing so you will need to decide what part of speech each nonsense word is. For instance, what part of speech often follows determiners like *the*? What part of speech may stand between the determiner and this other word? What part of speech often ends in *-y, -al, -ish,* or *-ous*? What part of speech often ends in *-ed* or *-ing*? Read your version of the poem to the class and defend your choice of words.

Exercise ten: Headlines and Telegrams. In English grammar, how important are function words like auxiliaries and determiners? Can we get along without them? If not, what kinds of communication problems occur when we try?

When we send telegrams, we use as few words as possible to state our message. Writers of newspaper headlines omit unnecessary words, too. In both cases ambiguity is possible. For example, SHIP SAILS TODAY has two possible meanings. They become clear when either determiners or auxiliaries are used. (Note that the auxiliary may change the form of its following verb.)

Determiner: SHIP THE SAILS TODAY   THE SHIP SAILS TODAY
Auxiliary: MUST SHIP SAILS TODAY   SHIP MUST SAIL TODAY

Here is a list of other telegrams and headlines that have two possible meanings. Figure out each of the two meanings by inserting determiners and auxiliaries.

1. BABY SWALLOWS FLY
2. KENNEDY REPORTS OPEN CONFERENCE
3. PROFESSOR BURNS LEAVES
4. RADIO BROADCASTS SMELL
5. PLAN MOVES LAST
6. NAVY WITNESSES SMOKE
7. STREET NEEDS CHANGE
8. GREASE SLIDES FAST
9. SWISS WATCHES STRIKE
10. SWALLOW DRINKS SLOWLY

Exercise eleven: Research on the Signal Systems of English. Three signal systems in English are function words, suffixes, and word order. In our analysis of telegrams and headlines we have already worked with function words. Suffixes are groups of sounds or letters that are attached to the end of words and serve to change their meanings. For instance, *-s* is attached to the singular noun *boy* to produce *boys* with the added meaning of plural; *-ed* is attached to the verb *play* to produce *played* with the added meaning of past.

Word order is the strongest signal system in English. We arrange the words of our sentences in a definite order. The most common English sentence order is noun-verb-noun.

Research has shown that by using these three signal systems we can make intelligent guesses about words that have been omitted from sentences. For instance, in the sentence "Cats meow and dogs ______," we can hardly avoid supplying "bark." Or in the sentence "Birds fly in the air and snakes ______ on the ground," we would almost certainly supply the verb "crawl." These facts reveal the power of English word order, which, with suffixes and function words, forms a powerful set of signal systems in English.

To test this power, here is the beginning of Stephen Crane's "The Open Boat." After their ship has sunk, four men are riding the waves in a small boat: the injured captain, a newspaper correspondent, the ship's cook, and the ship's oiler, Billie. In the story as it appears here every seventh word is omitted and replaced by a numbered blank. Use all the signals in the sentence to discover the exact word Crane used. Synonyms do not count. The answers are given at the end of the quotation, but there is no advantage in looking at them. We are testing the theory that a large percentage of the original words can be discovered from the clues given by the signal systems in the sentences.

The Open Boat

None of them knew the color [1] the sky. Their eyes glanced level, [2] were fastened upon the waves that [3] toward them. These waves were of [4] hue of slate, save for the [5], which were of foaming white, and [6] of the men knew the colors [7] the sea. The horizon narrowed and [8], and dipped and rose, and at [9] times its edge was jagged with [10] that seemed thrust up in points [11] rocks.

Many a man ought to [12] a bathtub larger than the boat [13] here rode upon the sea. These [14] were most wrongfully and barbarously abrupt [15] tall, and each froth-top was a [16] in small-boat navigation.

The cook squatted [17] the bottom, and looked with both [18] at the six inches of gunwale [19] separated him from the ocean. His [20] were rolled over his fat forearms, [21] the two flaps of his unbuttoned [22] dangled as he bent to bail [23] the boat. Often he said, "Gawd! [24] was a narrow clip." As he [25] it he invariably gazed eastward over [26] broken sea.

The oiler, steering with [27] of the two oars in the [28], sometimes raised himself suddenly to keep [29] of water that swirled in over [30] stern. It was a thin little [31], and it seemed often ready to [32].

The correspondent, pulling at the other [33], watched the waves and wondered why [34] was there.

The injured captain, lying [35] the bow, was at this time [36] in that profound dejection and indifference [37] comes, temporarily at least, to even [38] bravest and most enduring when, willy-nilly, [39] firm fails, the army loses, the [40] goes down. The mind of the [41] of a vessel is rooted deep [42] the timbers of her, though he [43] for a day or a decade; [44] this captain had on him the [45] impression of a scene in the [46] of dawn of seven turned faces, [47] later a stump of a topmast [48] a white ball on it, that [49] to and fro at the waves, [50] low and lower, and down. Thereafter [51] was something strange in his voice. [52] steady, it was deep with mourning, [53] of a quality beyond oration or [54].

"Keep 'er a little more south, [55]," said he.

"A little more south, [56]," said the oiler in the stern.

[57] seat in this boat was not [58] a seat upon a bucking bronco, [59], by the same token, a bronco [60] not much smaller. The craft pranced [61] reared and plunged like an animal. [62] each wave came, and she rose [63] it, she seemed like a horse [64] at a fence outrageously high. The [65] of her scramble over these walls [66] water is a mystic thing, and, [67], at the top of them were [68] these problems in white water, the [69] racing down from the summit of [70] wave requiring a new leap, and [71] leap from the air. Then, after [72] bumping a crest, she would slide [73] race and splash down a long [74], and arrive bobbing and nodding in [75] of the next menace.

Key

1. of	*9.* all	*17.* in	*25.* remarked
2. and	*10.* waves	*18.* eyes	*26.* the
3. swept	*11.* like	*19.* which	*27.* one
4. the	*12.* have	*20.* sleeves	*28.* boat
5. tops	*13.* which	*21.* and	*29.* clear
6. all	*14.* waves	*22.* vest	*30.* the
7. of	*15.* and	*23.* out	*31.* oar
8. widened	*16.* problem	*24.* that	*32.* snap

33. oar	*44.* and	*55.* Billie	*66.* of
34. he	*45.* stern	*56.* sir	*67.* moreover
35. in	*46.* grays	*57.* A	*68.* ordinarily
36. buried	*47.* and	*58.* unlike	*69.* foam
37. which	*48.* with	*59.* and	*70.* each
38. the	*49.* slashed	*60.* is	*71.* a
39. the	*50.* went	*61.* and	*72.* scornfully
40. ship	*51.* there	*62.* As	*73.* and
41. master	*52.* Although	*63.* for	*74.* incline
42. in	*53.* and	*64.* making	*75.* front
43. command	*54.* tears	*65.* manner	

After you have chosen a word for each blank and written it on your paper, compare your guesses with those of your classmates. On which blanks did everyone agree? Is there any way to explain this agreement? For instance, were prepositions especially easy to identify? Which blanks called forth the largest number of synonyms? If at any point you went completely off the track, analyze what caused this problem.

Take a paper you have previously written, and cut out every seventh word, leaving equally sized blanks in place of these words. Working with a partner, exchange papers and fill in each other's blanks. Both of you must choose exactly the word originally used. After this, analyze each other's fill-ins and present your findings in a two-minute oral report to the class. Use the questions after the story to generalize about the words that are missed. Do not simply stand up and read the list of missed words. This will not be interesting to your classmates.

CHAPTER THREE

Transformation of Sentences

INTRODUCTION

Look at these first five sentences of "The Killers," a short story by Ernest Hemingway. His sentence structure is often described as simple.

> The door of Henry's lunch-room opened and two men came in. They sat down at the counter.
>
> "What's yours?" George asked them.
>
> "I don't know," one of the men said. "What do you want to eat, Al?"

These sentences are very simple in structure, yet almost all show some complexity not present in our five basic sentence patterns. The first sentence contains two verbs, *opened* and *came,* as well as a double possessive, *of Henry's lunch-room.* These structures are not in our basic sentence patterns. The second sentence is an example of our first basic sentence pattern.

Noun Phrase/Subject +	**Intransitive Verb +**	**(Adverb)**
They	sat down	at the counter

The intransitive verb is a two-word verb. The third sentence, like the first, has two verbs, *is* and *asked,* and the first of these verbs is used in a question: *What's yours?* The basic sentence patterns show no questions. The fourth sentence also has two verbs, *know* and *said.* The first is used in a negative sentence: *I don't know.* No basic sentence pattern is negative. The last sentence has the name of one of the men, *Al,* used as a noun of direct address. The basic sentence patterns do not include this use of nouns.

In other words, most sentences are more complicated than basic sentences are. We hardly ever talk in basic sentences. Even preschool children use complicated sentence patterns. Listen to youngsters playing together—they ask questions, make negative statements, and string everything together with *and*'s. They know how to transform basic sentence patterns into many other patterns. They cannot explain how they perform these transformations, but they know how to do so. In this chapter we will analyze some English transformations. When we understand how they work, we can use them to increase our pleasure in reading and to write clearer sentences of interesting variety.

First, we study transformations that change sentences into other sentences. One related group of transformations produces questions, commands, negatives, ellipses, and passives. Another type of transformation ties sentences together by conjunction.

Second, we study transformations that change sentences into fragments. Fragments are pieces of sentences, ready to be inserted into other sentences. These fragments can be inserted into noun positions, adjective positions, or adverb positions in other sentences.

THE ARITHMETIC OF TRANSFORMATIONS

Transformations explain how sentences or parts of sentences may differ in form but agree in meaning. Apparently, we quickly learn that such relationships exist although we cannot explain our knowledge of them. For example, as suggested in Chapter Two, we know that the following word-groups are related because they all concern Bill and his captaincy.

1. They elected Bill captain.
2. Did they elect Bill captain?
3. When did they elect Bill captain?
4. Why did they elect Bill captain?
5. Where did they elect Bill captain?
6. They *did* elect Bill captain!
7. They did not elect Bill captain.
8. Bill was elected captain by them.
9. Their electing Bill captain . . .
10. Bill's being elected captain . . .
11. Bill's election as captain . . .
12. Bill, the captain, . . .

The first sentence, *They elected Bill captain,* combines two basic sentence patterns.

Basic Sentence Pattern 2:

N. Phrase/Subject + Trans. V. + N. Phrase/D. Obj. + (Adv.)

They elected Bill

Basic Sentence Pattern 4:

N. Phrase/Subject + Link. V. + N. Phrase/Pred. N. + (Adv.)

Bill was captain

We will compare the other word-groups with the first sentence.

The second sentence adds a word, *did.* The third, fourth, and fifth sentences keep the word *did* and add words beginning with the letters *w* and *h: when, why,* and *where.* Sentence 6 adds emphasis on *did,* and sentence 7 adds the word *not* after *did.* Sentence 8 does several things: it adds *was* and *by;* it moves *Bill* to the subject position in the sentence; and it changes *they* to *them* and moves it to the end of the sentence. The last four word-groups, 9 through 12, are not sentences; they are fragments ready to be inserted into another sentence. Comparing them to Sentence 1, observe how drastically they have been transformed.

Yet in spite of all the additions, subtractions, and rearrangements of words in these twelve word-groups, we know that the original meaning of the two basic sentences is still present. All the word-groups concern Bill and his captaincy. The transformations have not removed this meaning nor changed it in any important way.

These twelve word-groups are all *transforms*. All are produced by transformations. The first eight are sentences. In order to distinguish basic sentences from sentences produced by transformations, we call the latter *derived sentences*. Thus all sentences in the language are either basic sentences or derived sentences. If transformations have helped to produce them, they are derived sentences; if not, they are basic sentences.

Exercise one. To test the statement that we do not use basic sentences very often, study these four excerpts from four modern writers: Saul Bellow, Flannery O'Connor, Herman Wouk, and Joseph Conrad. Identify the basic sentences in each excerpt; each has at least one. The excerpt from Joseph Conrad's *Lord Jim* has four.

Then read a page in any short story or novel you like. How many basic sentences do you find? Compare two pages of the same short story or novel, one with a lot of conversation and the other with little or no conversation. Are there more basic sentences on the conversational page? Then compare two authors. Do you find that one uses a larger number of basic sentences than the other?

> He couldn't mention his children without boasting. In Wilhelm's opinion, there was little to boast of. Catherine, like Wilhelm, was big and fair-haired. She had married a court reporter who had a pretty hard time of it. She had taken a professional name, too—Philippa. At forty she was still ambitious to become a painter. Wilhelm didn't venture to criticize her work. It didn't do much to him, he said, but then he was no critic. Anyway, he and his sister were generally on the outs and he didn't often see her paintings. She worked very hard, but there were fifty thousand people in New York with paints and brushes, each practically a law unto himself. It was the Tower of Babel in paint. *He* didn't want to go far into this. Things were chaotic all over.
>
> From *Seize the Day*
> by Saul Bellow.

> The child upstairs had grown red in the face with excitement. She was kneeling down by the window so that only her eyes and forehead showed over the sill. Mrs. Cope told the

boys to come around on the other side of the house where the lawn chairs were and she led the way and Mrs. Pritchard followed. The child moved from the right bedroom across the hall and over into the left bedroom and looked down on the other side of the house where there were three white lawn chairs and a red hammock strung between two hazelnut trees. She was a pale fat girl of twelve with a frowning squint and a large mouth full of silver bands. She knelt down at the window.

From "A Circle in the Fire"
by Flannery O'Connor.

With a sense of great luxury and well-being, Willie crawled to the narrow upper bunk and slid between the fresh, rough Navy sheets. He lay only a few inches beneath the plates of the main deck. He had not much more room than he would have had under the lid of a coffin. A knotty valve of the fire main projected downward into his stomach. The stateroom was not as large as the dressing closet in his Manhasset home. But what did all that matter? From the clipping shack to this bunk was a great rise in the world. Willie closed his eyes, listened with pleasure to the hum of the ventilators, and felt in his bones the vibration of the main engines, transmitted through the springs of his bunk. The ship was alive again. He felt warm, and safe, and at home. Drowsiness came over him almost at once, and he slept deliciously.

From *The Caine Mutiny*
by Herman Wouk.

"Man the cutter!" Boys rushed past him. A coaster running in for shelter had crashed through a schooner at anchor, and one of the ship's instructors had seen the accident. A mob of boys clambered on the rails, clustered round the davits. "Collision. Just ahead of us. Mr. Symonds saw it." A push made him stagger against the mizzen-mast, and he caught hold of a rope. The old training-ship chained to her moorings quivered all over, bowing gently head to wind, and with her scanty rigging humming in a deep bass the breathless song of her youth at sea. "Lower away!" He saw the boat, manned, drop swiftly below the rail, and rushed after her. He heard a splash. "Let go; clear the falls!" He leaned over. The river alongside seethed in frothy streaks. The cutter could be seen in the falling darkness under the spell of tide and wind; that for a moment held her bound, and tossing abreast of the ship. A yelling voice in her reached him faintly: "Keep stroke, you young whelps, if you want to save anybody! Keep stroke!"

And suddenly she lifted high her bow, and, leaping with raised oars over a wave, broke the spell cast upon her by the wind and tide.

From *Lord Jim*
by Joseph Conrad.

TRANSFORMATIONS PRODUCING SENTENCES

One set of transformations that produces derived sentences works at the auxiliary position in the sentence. In a basic sentence, the auxiliary position is just in front of the main verb.

For example, sentences can be transformed into negatives by the addition of *not* or *n't* after the auxiliary.

Pepe should eat papaya.

becomes

Pepe should not eat papaya.

This is the *negative transformation.*

Sentences can be made shorter by subtracting words. In answer to

Who should eat papaya?

we can reply

Pepe should.

Here we omit everything that follows the auxiliary. This is the *ellipsis transformation. Ellipsis* means "omission."

Basic sentences can be transformed into commands by the subtraction of everything that precedes the verb—the subject and the auxiliary.

You will eat your tapioca pudding.

becomes

Eat your tapioca pudding.

This is the *imperative transformation. Imperative* means "command" or "order."

Sentences with transitive verbs can be made passive by adding *be* at the auxiliary position and changing the main verb to the past participle. The noun phrase serving as subject switches position with the noun phrase serving as direct object and the word *by* is added.

Pepe should eat papaya.

becomes

Papaya should be eaten by Pepe.

This is the *passive transformation.* Here are some other sentences of Basic Sentence Pattern 2 transformed by the passive transformation.

Nillion must own the diamond.
The diamond must be owned by Nillion.

Francine has studied trigonometry.
Trigonometry has been studied by Francine.

Mrs. Kaliforne writes many invitations.
Many invitations are written by Mrs. Kaliforne.

Byington is mailing the license today.
The license is being mailed today by Byington.

When sentences of Basic Sentence Pattern 3 undergo the passive transformation, two results are possible. The sentence

Francine gave Mary a letter.

becomes

A letter was given Mary by Francine.

or

Mary was given a letter by Francine.

In other words, either the direct object or the indirect object can move into the front position. When the direct object takes the front position, we would be more likely to say, "A letter was given to Mary by Francine."

Sentences can be transformed into questions by rearranging the auxiliary and the subject. This rearrangement creates interrogative word order.

Pepe should eat papaya.

becomes

Should Pepe eat papaya?

This is the *simple-question transformation.* It makes a question that can be answered by "Yes" or "No." Questions asking for more than a Yes/No reply are *information questions.* We can recognize information questions by the question word at their beginning. Since these words all contain *w* and *h,* we can refer to them as the *wh* words. Any part of our sentences can be questioned by a *wh* word. For example, take this Basic Sentence Pattern 2 sentence with three adverbs.

Pearl	will	toot	a horn	madly	at the game	tomorrow.
N. Phrase/ Subject	+ Aux.	+ Trans. Verb	+ N. Phrase/ D. Obj.	+ Adv. Manner	+ Adv. Place	+ Adv. Time

Putting this sentence into interrogative word order produces

Will Pearl toot a horn madly at the game tomorrow?

This is a simple question, which can be answered by "Yes" or "No." We can *wh* the whole sentence:

Why will Pearl toot a horn madly at the game tomorrow?

Now observe how we can question each element in the sentence by using different *wh* words.

First we can *wh* Pearl, the noun phrase serving as subject. The sentence transforms to

Who will toot a horn madly at the game tomorrow?

Next we can question the verb phrase, *will toot a horn:*

What will Pearl do madly at the game tomorrow?

Notice that *do* substitutes for *toot a horn.* We can also question a part of the verb phrase—its direct object, *a horn:*

What will Pearl toot madly at the game tomorrow?

We can leave in *horn* and *wh* only the article *a:*

What horn will Pearl toot madly at the game tomorrow?

or

Which horn will Pearl toot madly at the game tomorrow?

In the adverb positions, we can substitute *how* for *madly:*

How will Pearl toot a horn at the game tomorrow?

How is a *wh* word even though the *w* and *h* are inverted. We can substitute *where* for *at the game:*

Where will Pearl toot a horn madly tomorrow?

Finally, we can *wh tomorrow,* the time adverb:

When will Pearl toot a horn madly at the game?

All of these are examples of *wh-question transformations.*

The *wh* word that questions people is *who,* a word that has three forms: *who, whose,* and *whom. Who* questions a noun phrase serving as subject. *Whom* questions a noun phrase serving as indirect object, direct object, or object of a preposition. *Whose* questions a noun phrase showing possession. For example, we can apply the preceding facts to the sentence *Mr. Allardyce handed Gwen Joe's baby.*

Who handed Gwen Joe's baby? (Mr. Allardyce)
To whom did Mr. Allardyce hand Joe's baby? (Gwen)
Whose baby did Mr. Allardyce hand Gwen? (Joe's)
Whom did Mr. Allardyce hand Gwen? (Joe's baby)

None of the other *wh* words except *whoever* confronts us with the problem of choosing the correct form.

(Who, Whom) will play the Yanks tomorrow?
(Who, Whom) did he say was calling?
(Who, Whom) did Uncle George introduce?
(To who, To whom) did the class listen?

Here is a complete list of the *wh* words and their compounds in *-ever.*

who (whose, whom)	whoever (whosever, whomever)
which	whichever
what	whatever
when	whenever

where	wherever
how (and how much, how far, how long, how often)	however
why	whyever

In the sentence *What will Pearl do madly at the game tomorrow?* we saw *do* substituting for *toot a horn.* In this use, *do* is a "dummy verb," taking its meaning from the verb for which it substitutes. Suppose that instead of tooting a horn, Pearl was planning to wave a flag:

Pearl will wave a flag madly at the game tomorrow.

Then the *wh* transformation would produce:

What will Pearl do madly at the game tomorrow?

Now, however, the *do* replaces *wave a flag* instead of *toot a horn.*

Whenever the auxiliary of a verb phrase has no modal, *be,* or *have* in it, *do* enters the sentence as soon as we start transforming it. It carries tense, negative, emphasis, question or ellipsis. The sentence *Pepe eats papaya every day* can be transformed into:

Pepe does not eat papaya every day.
Pepe *does* eat papaya every day!
Does Pepe eat papaya every day?
Pepe does.

Of course, *do* is not always a dummy verb. It can be a regular transitive verb:

We do our work every day.

Exercise one. Make at least ten different questions from this sentence. In each case, describe how you made the transformation.

Dad bought Mother that pennant at the fair last month.

Exercise two. Transform each of these sentences into negative sentences and Yes/No questions.

1. The telegrapher has transmitted the signal.
2. A dog enjoys his fleas.
3. McIntosh removed the roadblock.
4. Snow White's stepmother is questioning the mirror.

Exercise three. Transform each of these sentences into an imperative.

1. You will throw out the lifeline.
2. You will separate the men from the boys.
3. You will guide the herd across the valley.
4. You will beat the bushwackers.
5. You will grind your teeth in unison.

Exercise four. Perform the passive transformation on these sentences.

1. Marshall tossed eggshells into the basket.
2. A loud scream drew Mrs. Quarlsby downstairs.
3. Juanito held a revolver in his left hand.
4. My folks bought the tickets yesterday.

Exercise five. Analyze the questions in these conversations from Ray Bradbury's "The Man Upstairs." List first the Yes/No questions and then the *wh* questions. But first, here are three of the questions not expressed in full:

"Ever see anything like it, Grandma?"
"About what?"
"Why?"

Expand each of these questions to its full form, using the context to help you.

Grandma was busy fingering a piecrust into a pan when Douglas entered the kitchen to place something on the table.

"Grandma, what's this?"

She glanced up briefly, over her glasses. "I don't know."

It was square, like a box, and elastic. It was bright orange in color. It had four square tubes, colored blue, attached to it. It smelled funny.

"Ever see anything like it, Grandma?"

"No."

"That's what *I* thought."

Douglas left it there, went from the kitchen. Five minutes later he returned with something else. "How about *this?*"

He laid down a bright pink linked chain with a purple triangle at one end.

"Don't bother me," said Grandma. "It's only a chain."

Next time he returned with two hands full. A ring, a square, a triangle, a pyramid, a rectangle, and—other shapes. All of them were pliable, resilient, and looked as if they were made of gelatin. "This isn't all," said Douglas, putting them down. "There's more where this came from."

Grandma said, "Yes, yes," in a far-off tone, very busy.

"You were wrong, Grandma."

"About what?"

"About all people being the same inside."

"Stop talking nonsense."

"Where's my piggy-bank?"

"On the mantel, where you left it."

"Thanks."

He tromped into the parlor, reached up for his piggy-bank.

Grandpa came home from the office at five.

"Grandpa, come upstairs."

"Sure, son. Why?"

"Something to show you. It's not nice; but it's interesting."

Grandpa chuckled following his grandson's feet up to Mr. Koberman's room.

"Grandma mustn't know about this; she wouldn't like it," said Douglas. He pushed the door wide open. "There."

Grandfather gasped.

From "The Man Upstairs"
by Ray Bradbury.

CONJUNCTION TRANSFORMATIONS

Conjunction transformations join two sentences to produce one sentence. The two sentences must have some words in common, a requirement of the conjunction transformation that can be presented by these two formulas:

$$X + Y + Z$$
$$X + W + Z$$

Each line represents a string of grammatical items. The only difference between the two lines is that the first line has Y at its center and the second line has W. To join these strings by a conjunction transformation, we remove the overlapping and insert a conjunction. For example, take these two sentences:

The strategy—of the coach—developed.
The strategy—of the team—developed.

In both sentences *the strategy* is the X element, and *developed* is the Z element. Y is *of the coach* and W is *of the team.* Using the conjunction transformation, we can join the two prepositional phrases—*of the coach* and *of the team*—to produce

The strategy of the coach and of the team developed.

Conjunctions are function words that tie together structures of equal grammatical weight: words, phrases, complete sentence patterns. *And* and *but* are the most common conjunctions, but a more complete list includes *or, nor, not, rather than, as well as,* and four pairs: *not only . . . but also, either . . . or, neither . . . nor,* and *both . . . and.*

Notice what happens when we try to join two elements of unequal grammatical weight.

The strategy—of the coach—developed.
The strategy—that they planned—developed.

The conjunction transformation produces this non-sentence:

*The strategy of the coach and that they planned developed.

In "Richard Cory," Edwin Arlington Robinson uses conjunction transformations effectively. He joins sentences to form compound sentences:

And he was always quietly arrayed,
And he was always human when he talked;

(The semicolon here is equivalent to a period.) He joins verbs to form compound predicates:

> Went home and put a bullet through his head.

He connects pairs of adjectives:

> Clean favored, and imperially slim.
> . . . rich . . . And admirably schooled . . .

Richard Cory

Whenever Richard Cory went down town,
    We people on the pavement looked at him:
He was a gentleman from sole to crown,
    Clean favored, and imperially slim.

And he was always quietly arrayed, 5
    And he was always human when he talked;
But still he fluttered pulses when he said,
    "Good-morning," and he glittered when he walked.

And he was rich—yes, richer than a king,
    And admirably schooled in every grace: 10
In fine, we thought that he was everything
    To make us wish that we were in his place.

So on we worked, and waited for the light,
    And went without the meat, and cursed the bread;
And Richard Cory, one calm summer night, 15
    Went home and put a bullet through his head.

Here is a sentence from *The Bear* by William Faulkner, describing the climax of Ike McCaslin's long search for the bear. It is interesting also because it shows Faulkner using conjunction transformations more complexly than Robinson did. Notice that in this long sentence there are only two *and*'s and one *but.* Commas stand in the places where another author might have used *or, and,* or *but.*

> It did not emerge, appear; it was just there, immobile, solid, fixed in the hot dappling of the green and windless noon, not as big as he had dreamed it, but as big as he had expected it, bigger, dimensionless, against the dappled obscurity, looking at him where he sat quietly on the log and looked back at it.

Mentally, we can expand the sentences that are joined and then reduced. "It did not emerge" and "It did not appear" become "It did not emerge, appear." After the semicolon there is a long sequence of words and word-groups that can be expanded to show their equal grammatical weight.

> It was just there. It was immobile. It was solid.
> It was fixed in the hot dappling of the green and windless noon.
> It was not as big as he had dreamed it.
> It was as big as he had expected it.
> It was bigger. It was dimensionless.
> It was against the dappled obscurity.
> It was looking at him where he sat quietly on the log and looked back at it.

That last sentence contains its own conjunction transformation, which puts together these two sentences: "He sat quietly on the log" and "He looked back at it."

Exercise one. Sort these grammatical items into two sets: prepositional phrases and sentences. Then put them together by conjunction transformations to produce four sensible sentences.

1. she stopped sobbing
2. in back of the table
3. Bill has had a beautiful romance this year
4. over the river
5. a red-faced man in a raincoat sat down beside her
6. they started talking nonsense
7. in front of the fireplace
8. let's go to Somerville next week
9. a red-faced man in a battered hat sat down beside her
10. Bill has had a terrible run of bad luck this year
11. through the woods

Exercise two. Write three sentences with compound subjects, three with compound predicates, and three compound sentences.

Exercise three. Here is Siegfried Sassoon's poem "Base Details." It contains seven *and*'s. We know that *and* connects items that are similar grammatically. In each case state the words connected by *and*. Then, by identifying their grammatical function, explain how these items are of equal grammatical weight. Where might other *and*'s be placed if this were prose and not poetry?

Base Details

If I were fierce, and bald, and short of breath,
    I'd live with scarlet Majors at the Base,
And speed glum heroes up the line to death.
    You'd see me with my puffy petulant face,
Guzzling and gulping in the best hotel, 5
    Reading the Roll of Honor. "Poor young chap,"
I'd say—"I used to know his father well;
    Yes, we've lost heavily in this last scrap."
And when the war is done and youth stone dead,
I'd toddle safely home and die—in bed. 10

Exercise four. Using the analysis of Faulkner's long sentence from *The Bear* as a guide, analyze this sentence by William Golding from *Lord of the Flies.* After expanding the reduced sentences, listing them, and studying them, write a sentence of your own modeled on Golding's.

> On the mountain-top the parachute filled and moved; the figure slid, rose to its feet, spun, swayed down through a vastness of wet air and trod with ungainly feet the tops of the high trees; falling, still falling, it sank toward the beach and the boys rushed screaming into the darkness.

TRANSFORMATIONS PRODUCING PIECES OF SENTENCES

When a transformation reduces a basic sentence to a piece of a sentence, that transform can no longer stand as a complete sentence but must be inserted into another sentence. It has become a possible *insert*. The sentence into which it is inserted is the *receiver*. For instance, the basic sentence *Herman winked at her* can be transformed into . . . *Herman to wink at her* . . . or . . . *Herman's winking at her.* These transforms are no longer complete sentences. They are fragments ready to be inserted into another sentence, the receiver.

All of these examples include some form of the sentence *Herman winked at her.*

They are waiting for Herman to wink at her.
For Herman to wink at her is foolish.
It is foolish for Herman to wink at her.
The reason for Herman's winking at her is amazing.
Herman's winking at her makes us sad.
We hate to think about Herman's winking at her.

If we start with the sentence *John is a fool,* it can be transformed into . . . *John to be a fool* . . . or . . . *John being a fool* . . . .

John is foolish can be transformed into . . . *John to be foolish* . . . or . . . *John being foolish* . . . .

The counterspy found the hidden mike can be transformed into . . . *the counterspy to find the hidden mike* . . . or . . . *the counterspy finding the hidden mike* . . . .

Since these transformations are only pieces of sentences, they must be inserted into receivers. The receiver determines which form of the insert we use. For instance, we can add *Rudolph stepped into the limousine* to *The thugs persuaded Rudolph* by transforming the first sentence into a form that fits with *persuaded:*

The thugs persuaded Rudolph to step into the limousine.

Change *persuaded* to *caught:*

The thugs caught Rudolph stepping into the limousine.

Change *caught* to *prevented:*

The thugs prevented Rudolph from stepping into the limousine.

Certain adjectives too can accept inserts. For example, take these two sentences:

The puzzle was simple.
He solved the puzzle.

These can combine to produce either *The puzzle was simple to solve* or *The puzzle was simple for him to solve.*

Any sentence can be either an insert or a receiver. That is, all sentences have positions that can be filled by inserts, and all sentences can themselves be transformed into inserts. These transformations illustrate how we make complex sentences from basic sentences.

Exercise one. Below is a list of some other adjectives that can accept inserts of various forms. As fluent speakers of English, we know which inserts fit with which adjectives. For example, if we wish to insert the sentence *He skied* after the adjective *clever,* we can transform it into the present participle form and insert it to produce:

He is clever at skiing.

or

He is clever in skiing.

or

He is clever about skiing.

but not

*He is clever from skiing.

or

*He is clever for skiing.

We can also transform *He skied* into an infinitive, *to ski,* and insert it after *clever.*

He is clever to ski.

as in the sentence, "If he expects to reach the lodge before nightfall, he is clever to ski down the mountain early in the afternoon."

Make sentences using the following adjectives and follow them by suitable inserts.

eager	ready
skillful	happy
difficult	undecided
certain	successful

Exercise two. Write one sentence using each of these verbs in the receiver and following it by an insert. Examples:

Receiver: I can *imagine* it.

He is going.	I am going.
I can imagine him going.	I can imagine going.

believe	appoint
find	imagine
force	begin
refuse	recognize
prefer	want

Exercise three. Write one long sentence using as many of the following verbs as possible. Example: I *persuaded* him to *keep trying* to *refrain* from *convincing* her to *avoid preventing* Bill from *refusing* . . . and so on.

keep	put	want
expect	prevent	refrain
persuade	force	avoid
begin	find	catch
imagine	prefer	

Nominalization

All sentences can be nominalized; that is, they can be transformed into noun-like inserts, or *nominals.* We will examine five main ways to transform sentences into nominals.

1. Place *that* before any sentence and it becomes a nominal.

The pitcher refused.
 becomes . . . that the pitcher refused . . .

Smith hit the sergeant.
 becomes . . . that Smith hit the sergeant . . .

My buddy was innocent.
 becomes . . . that my buddy was innocent . . .

2. Use the battery of *wh* question words to produce nominals. When we use the *wh* words in this way, the word order

stays normal; it does not become interrogative with the auxiliary changing position with the subject.

He shook his fist.
  becomes . . . what he shook . . .
He looked hunted.
  becomes . . . how he looked . . .
Jeff put his hands over his face.
  becomes . . . where Jeff put his hands . . .

3. Transform the inserts into *-ing* forms, which are called *gerunds*. When the inserts are transformed into gerunds, notice that the subject adopts the possessive form. *He* becomes *his, she* becomes *her, wolf* becomes *wolf's*.

He felt ferocious.
  becomes . . . his feeling ferocious . . .
She followed the raft.
  becomes . . . her following the raft . . .
The wolf howled weirdly.
  becomes . . . the wolf's howling weirdly . . .

4. Transform the inserts into infinitives.

The trapdoor opened.
  becomes . . . for the trapdoor to open . . .
He stumbled to the rail.
  becomes . . . for him to stumble to the rail . . .
The log blazed fiercely.
  becomes . . . for the log to blaze fiercely . . .

If we leave out the subject, the *for* disappears, too, leaving only the *to*, the marker of the infinitive.

. . . to stumble to the rail . . .   . . . to blaze fiercely . . .

5. Use a noun that equates with the verb of the insert. Not all verbs have a related noun form.

Phil claimed victory.
  becomes . . . Phil's claim of victory . . .
The team refused the penalty.
  becomes . . . the team's refusal of the penalty . . .
Egbert is mad.
  becomes . . . Egbert's madness . . .

She feared cancer.
becomes . . . her fear of cancer . . .

These nominals can be inserted into noun positions in receivers. The noun positions, however, must not already be filled by nouns. Instead, they must be filled by the dummy position markers *someone* or *something*. These dummy markers indicate positions in the receiver that can be filled by nominal inserts: subject position, object position, and position after prepositions. Here are some receivers:

{Something / Someone} was unusual.

{Something / Someone} pleased me.

{Something / Someone} was a shock.

{Something / Someone} concerned us all.

I told her {something. / someone.}

I knew {something. / someone.}

We approved of {something. / someone.}

I complained about {something. / someone.}

These receivers can accept various nominal inserts, although not every nominal fits into every receiver.

That the pitcher refused was unusual.
That my buddy was innocent pleased me.
For the trapdoor to open was a shock.
How he looked concerned us all.
I told her how he looked.
I told her who he was.
I knew that Smith hit the sergeant.
We approved of the home team's refusal of the penalty.
I complained about her following the raft.
I complained about how he looked.

Exercise four. Write five other derived sentences using the nominal inserts and the receivers in your text.

Exercise five. Nominalize each of the following basic sentences in four or five ways, and then insert them into the noun positions in the accompanying receivers. These positions are marked by the dummy marker *something.* Here are the receivers:

Frank noticed something.
Something amazed the defense attorney.

Example: Sentence to be transformed and inserted into a receiver:

Mary knocked at the door.

Frank noticed that Mary knocked at the door.
Frank noticed how Mary knocked at the door.
Frank noticed Mary's knocking at the door.
Frank noticed Mary's knock at the door.

Here are the basic sentences to be transformed and inserted:

1. The walls collapsed.
2. David feared her agony.
3. Glenn glanced at the retrorockets.
4. Albert was a gentleman.
5. The danger was visible.

Adjectivalization

In the nursery rhyme "The House that Jack Built" a sentence is made longer and longer by the progressive inserting of one transform into another. Starting with two basic sentences:

This is the house.
Jack built the house.

we see that we are talking about the same house in both sentences, which is a signal that the adjectivalization transformation is permitted. We substitute *that* for *the house* in the second sentence and move it to the front where it links the two sentences:

This is the house that Jack built.

Then two more sentences:

This is the malt.
The malt lay in the house.

combine to form

This is the malt that lay in the house.

Now the word *house* appears in that sentence and in

This is the house that Jack built.

We can put them together to get

This is the malt that lay in the house that Jack built.

The nursery rhyme continues:

This is the rat that ate the malt that lay in the house that Jack built.

This is the cat that killed the rat that ate the malt that lay in the house that Jack built.

This is the dog that worried the cat that killed the rat that ate the malt that lay in the house that Jack built.

This is the cow with the crumpled horn that tossed the dog that worried the cat that killed the rat that ate the malt that lay in the house that Jack built.

This is the maiden all forlorn that milked the cow with the crumpled horn that tossed the dog that worried the cat that killed the rat that ate the malt that lay in the house that Jack built.

This is the man all tattered and torn that kissed the maiden all forlorn that milked the cow with the crumpled horn that tossed the dog that worried the cat that killed the rat that ate the malt that lay in the house that Jack built.

This is the preacher all shaven and shorn that married the man all tattered and torn that kissed the maiden all forlorn that milked the cow with the crumpled horn that tossed the dog that worried the cat that killed the rat that ate the malt that lay in the house that Jack built.

This nursery rhyme shows how insertion transformations can pile up to produce very long sentences. You could easily add to the story. It also illustrates adjectivalization transformation, the transformation of sentences into adjective-like transforms ready for insertion in front of or following a noun. The important fact is that by means of relative clauses—inserts beginning with *who, which,* or *that*—we can produce an infinite set of noun modifiers. All nouns can accept modifiers on either side.

$$\left.\begin{array}{l}\text{Modifier}\\ \text{Position}\end{array}\right\} \text{ NOUN } \left\{\begin{array}{l}\text{Modifier}\\ \text{Position}\end{array}\right.$$

The position chosen depends on the length of the modifier, which may be a complete relative clause, a phrase, or a single word.

Complete relative clauses. Any sentence can be transformed into a relative clause. Any relative clause can be inserted into a receiver with which it shares a noun. For example:

Frank bought Mary a pizza pie.
The pizza pie burned her tongue.

become either

Frank bought Mary a pizza pie which burned her tongue.

or

The pizza pie which Frank bought Mary burned her tongue.

Sentences such as

The bear was shot by the hunter.
The bear was losing blood fast.

become either

The bear which was shot by the hunter was losing blood fast.

or

The bear which was losing blood fast was shot by the hunter.

The quartet was singing the song.
The song had been written by Bill Smith.

become either

The quartet was singing the song which had been written by Bill Smith.

or

The song which the quartet was singing had been written by Bill Smith.

The missile is in the air.
The missile was launched from the ground.

become either

The missile which was launched from the ground is in the air.

or

The missile which is in the air was launched from the ground.

The seniors are watching the movie.
The movie is a western.

become either

The seniors are watching the movie which is a western.

or

The movie which the seniors are watching is a western.

The canoeist was shooting the rapids.
The rapids were swirling wildly.

become either

The canoeist was shooting the rapids which were swirling wildly.

or

The rapids which the canoeist was shooting were swirling wildly.

The starlet is charming.
The starlet is working hard.

become either

The starlet who is charming is working hard.

or

The starlet who is working hard is charming.

The second baseman broke records.
The second baseman was honored at the banquet.

become either

The second baseman who broke records was honored at the banquet.

or

The second baseman who was honored at the banquet broke records.

The plane is a fighter.
The plane is making an emergency landing.

become either

The plane which is making an emergency landing is a fighter.

or

The plane which is a fighter is making an emergency landing.

The truck is burning oil.
The truck is a diesel.

become either

The truck which is burning oil is a diesel.

or

The truck which is a diesel is burning oil.

Some of these transformations produce awkward, wordy sentences. We will soon see how they can be tightened by reducing the relative clauses.

In these transforms, the *who*'s and *which*'s certainly look like *wh* question words. But they are not working like *wh* question words. They appear at the front of transforms to be inserted into receivers, not in front of questions that can stand alone as sentences. These transforms must be inserted into receivers. Here *who* and *which* are relatives, and the whole insert is called a *relative clause.*

Go back through the transforms now and try changing the *which*'s to *that*'s. Notice that the change makes some of the sentences sound less awkward. Then try omitting the *that*'s. You will discover that you can omit *that* when it replaces a direct object in the original sentence.

Now look at this pair of sentences where another kind of object is involved—the object of a preposition, *against.*

The bill lost by a big margin.
The senator voted against the bill.

If we combine these sentences in writing, the result may be

The bill against which the senator voted lost by a big margin.

In speech, our sentence may well be

The bill that the senator voted against lost by a big margin.

or, omitting *that,*

The bill the senator voted against lost by a big margin.

Standard English use of *which* or *that* is often influenced by whether we are writing or speaking.

Professional writers frequently prefer *which* or *that,* one or the other. In filling the blanks in Crane's "The Open Boat," perhaps you observed that he preferred *which* in three places where he could as well have used *that.* Be on the lookout to observe the choices of other writers.

Phrases. Many relative clauses containing *be,* either as an auxiliary or as a main verb, can be reduced to phrases by the subtraction of the relative and *be.*

For example, from the transforms above, we can reduce

The bear which was shot by the hunter was losing blood fast.

to

The bear shot by the hunter was losing blood fast.

We can reduce its partner

The bear which was losing blood fast was shot by the hunter.

to

The bear losing blood fast was shot by the hunter.

Go through the other complete relative clauses above, eliminating the relative and the various forms of *be,* to discover other possible reductions. If this reduction leaves only one word from the relative clause, where do you put it in the sentence?

Perhaps you have wanted to place commas around some of the relative clauses we have been discussing. Indeed, when the sentences appear alone, without context to clarify their meaning, they could be written either with or without commas. Without commas they are called *restrictive* relative clauses; with commas they are called *appositive* relative clauses. When relative clauses are preceded by proper nouns—nouns referring to specific persons or things and always capitalized in writing—we must use commas. Look at these sentences:

They admired Mr. Milquetoast, who is the father of the bride.
My hometown is Chicago, which is a really big city.
Jane Redstone, who is my uncle's wife, left for Seattle.

Each relative clause is punctuated by commas. They are appositive relative clauses. We can reduce them by the omission of the relative and *be.*

They admired Mr. Milquetoast, the father of the bride.
My hometown is Chicago, a really big town.
Jane Redstone, my uncle's wife, left for Seattle.

The resulting phrases are called *appositives.*

Single-word modifiers. Some phrases reduce to single-word modifiers. Some complete relative clauses skip the phrase stage and reduce directly to single-word modifiers. In either case, the single-word modifier must move to the position in front of the noun.

The plane, a fighter . . .
becomes The fighter plane . . .
The truck, a diesel . . .
becomes The diesel truck . . .
The starlet who is charming . . .
becomes The charming starlet . . .

Sometimes the form or order of the words changes with the reduction to the single-word modifier.

The truck, burning oil . . .
becomes The oil-burning truck . . .
The second baseman who broke records . . .
becomes The record-breaking second baseman . . .

The verb *have* (not the auxiliary *have*) behaves interestingly under transformation. From these three sentences

The cadet had a cold.
The cold kept him in the hospital.
The cadet felt sick.

we can observe how the three versions of the possessive transformation work. *The cadet had a cold* transforms to *the cadet's cold* and can then be inserted into *The cold kept him in the hospital* to produce:

The cadet's cold kept him in the hospital.

The cadet had a cold also transforms into *the cadet with a cold* and can be inserted into *The cadet felt sick* to produce:

The cadet with a cold felt sick.

Of course, single-word modifiers can themselves be modified. Then they are *headwords* and still work as single-word modifiers.

. . . the dim sidewalks . . .
can be . . . the very dim sidewalks . . .

. . . the trotting horse . . .
can be . . . the fast trotting horse . . .

Exercise six. Here are some derived sentences. First, pick out the relative clauses that cannot reduce. Then, reduce the others to either a phrase or a single word (or a single headword with its modifiers). Show each stage.

1. The man who had been threatening the crowd surrendered his weapon.
2. The team that won jumped the gun.
3. The investigator called the ambulance, which hit a tree.
4. People pass silently at night on sidewalks which are shrouded in fog.
5. The Mustang, which had plunged off the road, turned half-over.
6. My mountain cabin, which is rather small, is quite comfortable.
7. My father, who is a baseball player, goes to college in the winter.
8. They laughed at the worried frown which was twisting his face.
9. They negotiated the turn, which was very sharp.
10. The boy who is at the ballpark hopes to catch a foul.

Exercise seven. The inserts in these sentences have been reduced to single-word modifiers or phrases. By stages expand them to their full relative clauses. Then write the basic sentence from which they come.

1. My very young mother loves me dearly.
2. The Buffalo Bills, a barbershop quartet, sang in the movie.
3. The cold water licked their ankles.
4. Jim, quaking in his socks, hit Hartmann in the eye.
5. Mr. Emiscan's cold kept him out for two weeks.
6. She saw the photograph of the old woman.
7. She woke up with a happy feeling.
8. Lois had a line of amusing gossip.
9. Mrs. Browning was reading in a rather soothing voice.
10. The door of the taxi was yellow.

Exercise eight. Perform the three possessive transformations on each of these sentences to produce inserts.

1. The room has two broken windows.
2. The bus driver has an orange cap.
3. A girl has common sense.
4. His big car had snow tires.

Exercise nine. Perform the apposition transformation on these sentences to produce inserts.

1. Betty is the Orchard Queen.
2. The Falcons are the losers in the fifty-yard dash.
3. Richard Cory was a scholar and a gentleman.

Adverbialization

All sentences can be adverbialized. That is, they can be changed into adverb-like transforms or adverbials, which can then be inserted into receivers in adverb positions. A sentence is transformed into an adverbial by the addition of a subordinating conjunction, or subordinator. Here is a list of some subordinators:

after	for	unless
although	if	when
because	since	while
before	though	as

These transforms can be inserted into a receiver in any of the adverb positions.

$$\left\{\begin{matrix}\text{Adverb}\\ \text{Position}\end{matrix}\right\} \text{ Noun Phrase } \left\{\begin{matrix}\text{Adverb}\\ \text{Position}\end{matrix}\right\} \text{ Verb Phrase } \left\{\begin{matrix}\text{Adverb}\\ \text{Position}\end{matrix}\right\}$$

When they noticed Tom, the boys stopped to watch him paint.
The boys, when they noticed Tom, stopped to watch him paint.
The boys stopped to watch him paint when they noticed Tom.

As the car pulled away, she sat there terribly alone.
She sat there, as the car pulled away, terribly alone.
She sat there terribly alone as the car pulled away.

After lightning gashed the dark sky, the thing crawled out of the forest.

The thing, after lightning gashed the dark sky, crawled out of the forest.
The thing crawled out of the forest after lightning gashed the dark sky.

We can turn these two sentence patterns around, making the insert the receiver.

After the thing crawled out of the forest, lightning gashed the dark sky.
Lightning, after the thing crawled out of the forest, gashed the dark sky.
Lightning gashed the dark sky after the thing crawled out of the forest.

Adverbial inserts can reduce under certain conditions.

1. If the subordinator is *while* or *when,* a sentence like

While (when) he was reading the newspaper, he relaxed.

can omit the *he* and *was* to become

While (when) reading the newspaper, he relaxed.

Further, it can lose the *while* or *when* to become

Reading the newspaper, he relaxed.

2. If the adverbial insert has a subject different from that of its receiver, it can reduce to an absolute. In absolutes the subordinator disappears and the verb stands in the present participle or the past participle. If the verb of the insert is *be,* it too disappears. Here are some examples.

Full adverbial insert:
His eyes widened with delight, *as his laughter echoed down the hall.*

Absolute:
His eyes widened with delight, *his laughter echoing down the hall.*

Full adverbial insert:
The intern frowned again, *because his ambulance was delayed by heavy traffic.*

Absolute:
The intern frowned again, *his ambulance delayed by heavy traffic.*

Full adverbial insert:
Lady Joan gossiped constantly, *although her words were gentle and cool.*

Absolute:
Lady Joan gossiped constantly, *her words gentle and cool.*

Exercise ten. Write ten sentences. Make five of them adverbial transforms by adding subordinators. Insert them into the other five sentences at the three adverb positions.

Exercise eleven. Expand the absolutes in the following sentences to full adverbial inserts.

1. Philip tried to start the car again, *his breath hissing through his clenched teeth, his bruised hands struggling to stop shaking, his eyes gray with terror.*
2. We had a happy Christmas that year, *gifts under the tree, our stockings stuffed with goodies, the table groaning under its load of succulent food.*
3. The Wilsons lay in their deck chairs, *their eyes puckered against the brilliant sun, their feet encased in plastic sandals, dreams of happy days ahead filling their drowsy heads.*

Exercise twelve. Reduce the adverbial inserts in the following sentences to absolutes.

1. He spoke sweetly and quietly, *while his hands folded and unfolded nervously over the axhandle.*
2. I climbed the lonely hill, *as my head ached with fear and suspicion.*
3. Rose is standing near the bedroom door, *while the coffee bubbles in the kitchen.*
4. They danced uncertainly at first, *because Bob was unsure of his balance and Liz was trying to make him confident.*
5. She read the letter quickly, *as her lips parted with joy, her head tilted back, and a bright blush tinged her cheeks.*

Summary Exercises

Exercise one. Each group below contains pieces of scrambled sentences, two sentences in each group. The same basic sentence pattern underlies both sentences in each group. Unscramble each group to form the two sentences it contains, figure out the underlying basic sentence pattern by removing the inserts, and explain why it is that pattern.[1]

1. by the day after tomorrow — their voices — your new sweater — strangely hoarse — will be — since last year — almost half-done — have become
2. was sprinting — the racing stables — from midnight until dawn — toward the finish line — were burning — the long-distance runner
3. have forwarded — her other dolls — Warner and his brother — some long over-due dresses — the governor — is making — Beulah Belinda — his walnut gavel
4. the uniformed detective — ominous cracklings — the glaring light — was following — in the dark — the forward observers — with hypnotized eyes — were hearing
5. a weak-kneed constable — the secret of her success — must be — the elder Mr. Halsey — the rugs on Mrs. Crickton's floors — have been

Exercise two. Study these two paragraphs by John Steinbeck and Ray Bradbury to reach conclusions about their use of conjunction transformations and adverbialization transformations. Remember that the most common signals of conjunction transformations are *and, but,* and *or.* The most common signals of adverbialization transformations are the subordinators listed on page 133. Which type do these authors prefer? Do they differ from each other in their preference?

> The neighbors were tumbling from their houses now, and they watched the falling sparks and stamped them out to save their own houses. Suddenly Kino was afraid. The light made him afraid. He remembered the man lying dead in the brush beside the path, and he took Juana by the arm and drew her into the shadow of a house away from the light, for light was danger to him. For a moment he considered and then he worked among the shadows until he came to the house of Juan Tomás, his brother, and he slipped into the doorway and drew Juana after him. Outside, he could hear the squeal of children and the shouts of the neighbors, for his friends thought he might be inside the burning house.

From *The Pearl*
by John Steinbeck.

---

[1] This exercise was suggested by Problem Two, pp. 130-132 in John C. Mellon's *The Grammar of English Sentences* (Culver, Indiana: Culver Military Academy, 1964).

He was rather shocked, but not surprised, somehow, when the truck came rolling out of an alley straight at him. He was just congratulating himself on his keen sense of observation and talking out what he would say to the police in his mind, when the truck smashed into his car. It wasn't really his car, that was the disheartening thing about it. In a preoccupied mood he was tossed first this way and then that way, while he thought, what a shame, Morgan has gone and lent me his extra car for a few days until my other car is fixed, and now here I go again. The windshield hammered back into his face. He was forced back and forth in several lightning jerks. Then all motion stopped and all noise stopped and only pain filled him up.

From "The Crowd"
by Ray Bradbury.

Exercise three. Read this paragraph by James Michener to observe his frequent use of adjectivalization transformations. List all the relative clauses and reduced relative clauses that you find. Compare Michener's use of transformations with that of Steinbeck and Bradbury in the preceding exercise. Does Michener here use adverbialization transformations? Conjunction transformations?

A communist bullet no bigger than a man's thumb, fired at random by some ground defender of the dump, had blundered haphazardly into the turbine blades, which were then whirring at nearly 13,000 revolutions a minute. So delicately was the jet engine balanced that the loss of only two blade tips had thrown the entire mechanism out of balance, and the grinding noise Brubaker heard was the turbine throwing off dozens of knifelike blades which slashed into the fuselage or out through the dark sky. Like the society which had conceived the engine, the turbine was of such advanced construction that even trivial disruption of one fundamental part endangered the entire structure.

From *The Bridges at Toko-Ri*
by James A. Michener.

CHAPTER FOUR

Sentences and Non-sentences

Even though transformations produce extremely complicated sentences, we recognize easily that they are grammatical. They "sound right" to us. We can write our own sentences using them as models. In this chapter we will see that we can just as easily recognize non-sentences in English—those word-groups that native speakers of English would never say, although foreigners might. Then we will see how poets stretch and manipulate English grammar to interesting extremes without producing non-sentences.

FOREIGNERS

Three friends, Carlos Gonzales, Katsuko Kobayashi, and Jonathan Yankey, have just finished reading "The Very Proper Gander" by James Thurber. Read this story and then their conversation about it.

The Very Proper Gander

Not so very long ago there was a very fine gander. He was strong and smooth and beautiful and he spent most of his time singing to his wife and children. One day somebody who saw him strutting up and down in his yard and singing remarked, "There is a very proper gander." An old hen overheard this and told her husband about it that night in the roost. "They said something about propaganda," she said. "I have always suspected that," said the rooster, and he went around the barnyard next day telling everybody that the very fine gander was a dangerous bird, more than likely a hawk in gander's clothing. A small brown hen remembered a time when at a great distance she had seen the gander talking with some hawks in the forest. "They were up to no good," she said. A duck remembered that the gander had once told him he did not believe in anything. "He said to hell with the flag, too," said the duck. A guinea hen recalled that she had once seen somebody who looked very much like the gander throw something that looked a great deal like a bomb. Finally everybody snatched up sticks and stones and descended on the gander's house. He was strutting in his front yard, singing to his children and his wife. "There he is!" everybody cried. "Hawk-lover! Unbeliever! Flag-hater! Bomb-thrower!" So they set upon him and drove him out of the country.

MORAL: Anybody who you or your wife thinks is going to overthrow the government by violence must be driven out of the country.

"Here we have the much that can be done by propaganda," Carlos began. "The gander was the big and powerful among the rest of the animals. He was beautiful and peaceful to be driven out of his home and his country. The brown hen and his husband, the old rooster, were in this case the proper ones to be driven out of the country, because they started the propaganda against the good gander. We could possibly realized that we should drive the rooster and her wife, the hen, the next time."

"The meaning for me is not quite same," Katsuko said. "The moral is ironic. It tells that if somebody has different thinkings from other people in a same community, he holds a dangerous propaganda. He has to go to another place because he disturbed his community with doing something which differs from other people do. This fable reminded me one proverb: 'When in Rome do as a Roman do.' Actually the moral itself is a strong propaganda. It criticizes a society where a panic about propaganda becomes itself a powerful propaganda. In other words, by calling something propaganda, one can make a powerful propaganda."

"I certainly agree more with you, Katsuko, than with Carlos," said Jonathan. "I don't think Thurber means that either group should be driven out. In a democracy all citizens are guaranteed freedom of speech, freedom against unreasonable search and seizure, freedom from cruel and unusual punishment, and a speedy trial. However, if anyone advocates the overthrow of the government by force, he is guilty of treason, and that is punishable by death. The poor old gander was falsely accused of treason, denied all his rights, and driven out of his country without a trial. So, ironically, putting down suspected treason involved breaking the most basic rules of democracy."

Carlos and Katsuko are two foreign speakers of English. Spanish is Carlos's native language, and Japanese is Katsuko's. Jonathan is a native speaker of English. Although Jonathan can understand the English spoken by his two friends, they prove they are foreigners by producing several non-sentences—word-groups that no native speaker of English would say. Katsuko's non-sentences are not identical with Carlos's non-sentences, however. They differ because Katsuko has a Japanese grammar-machine built into her head, while Carlos has a Spanish grammar-machine built into his.

For example, although they both have trouble with determiners, Katsuko has special difficulties with articles, while Carlos has more problems with possessives. Japanese has no articles, and therefore Katsuko uses English articles in strange, unexpected ways. Sometimes she omits them where English requires them, as in "The meaning for me is not quite same." We would say, ". . . not quite *the* same." Sometimes she chooses the wrong article as in ". . . *a* same community." We would say, ". . . *the* same community." At still other times she seems to treat articles inconsistently. She inserts *a* before *propaganda* several times—a position in which we would never use *a*—but at other times she omits *a* and uses *propaganda* without an article as we would. Perhaps, however, we can discover a consistent pattern of error beneath her apparently inconsistent language behavior. List each context in which she uses *propaganda* and compare these contexts. What do you discover? How would you explain Katsuko's mistakes to her if you wanted to help her speak English more accurately?

Carlos, on the other hand, has a different kind of determiner trouble. He misuses the possessives *his* and *her*. In Spanish such words agree in gender with the noun they modify. Therefore, Carlos says "his husband" and "her wife" because *husband* is masculine and *wife* is feminine. In English, however, we say "her husband" because *her* refers to the feminine *hen* and "his wife" because *his* refers to the masculine *rooster*.

Exercise one. Examine the speeches of Carlos and Katsuko and list the non-sentences you find. Then rephrase these word-groups to make them English sentences. Notice that it is not very difficult to figure out the meaning of the non-sentences.

POETS

Although foreigners often produce non-sentences in English, native speakers do not. Poets may stretch the grammar of the language boldly, but never to the point of being completely ungrammatical. Starting with Robert Browning's "Pippa's Song" from "Pippa Passes," and continuing through Robert Frost's "A Prayer in Spring," E. E. Cummings' "Spring is like a perhaps hand," and Gerard Manley Hopkins' "Spring," you will see that each poem increases the strain on the grammar. Although we have to work harder and harder to fit their language into the grammar of English, in each case we can do so. They are writing strange English sentences, but they are not writing non-sentences.

First, here is Robert Browning's completely grammatical "Pippa's Song."

> The year's at the spring,
> And day's at the morn;
> Morning's at seven;
> The hill-side's dew-pearl'd;
> The lark's on the wing; 5
> The snail's on the thorn:
> God's in His heaven—
> All's right with the world!

We know that this is a poem. It has rhythm and rhyme—*spring–wing, morn–thorn, seven–heaven,* and *pearl'd–world.* It uses metaphor—dew is compared to pearls. Lastly, the prosaic verb *to fly* becomes the poetical *to be on the wing.* However, the grammar of the poem is straightforward and normal. The words stand in their expected positions. The sentence patterns are uniform and simple—a noun phrase followed by *is* followed by a prepositional phrase, *at the spring, at the morn, on the wing, on the thorn, in his heaven,* or by an adjective, *dew-pearl'd,* or by both, *right with the world.*

"A Prayer in Spring," by Robert Frost, is somewhat less grammatical than Browning's "Pippa's Song," although rhythm and rhyme are quite clear.

A Prayer in Spring

> Oh, give us pleasure in the flowers today;
> And give us not to think so far away
> As the uncertain harvest; keep us here
> All simply in the springing of the year.

Oh, give us pleasure in the orchard white, 5
Like nothing else by day, like ghosts by night;
And make us happy in the happy bees,
The swarm dilating round the perfect trees.

And make us happy in the darting bird
That suddenly above the bees is heard, 10
The meteor that thrusts in with needle bill,
And off a blossom in midair stands still.

For this is love and nothing else is love,
The which it is reserved for God above
To sanctify to what far ends He will, 15
But which it only needs that we fulfill.

Frost uses prayer style, in which the subject of the sentence is not normally expressed. Each sentence starts with the verb or with *Oh,* another characteristic of the style. However, notice that Frost distorts the normal word order of English in several places. For instance, *give us not to think* is less grammatical than *do not let us think,* which we would use in normal conversation. In modern English, the dummy verb *do* always appears in this kind of sentence. Also, *the orchard white* presents an abnormal word order; normal English word order is determiner-adjective-noun, not determiner-noun-adjective. Frost obviously chose this order so that *white* would rhyme with *night* in the next line. Again the word order is distorted in *off a blossom in midair stands still.* More strictly grammatical word order is *stands still in midair off a blossom.* Frost is not wrong or misguided because of these distortions. Such tensions challenge and delight the intelligent reader.

"Spring is like a perhaps hand," by E. E. Cummings, looks strange because of its unusual punctuation, capitalization, and parentheses. Read it aloud several times, listening to it carefully.

Spring is like a perhaps hand

Spring is like a perhaps hand
(which comes carefully
out of Nowhere)arranging
a window,into which people look (while
people stare 5
arranging and changing placing
carefully there a strange
thing and a known thing here) and

changing everything carefully

spring is like a perhaps 10
Hand in a window
(carefully to
and fro moving New and
Old things,while
people stare carefully 15
moving a perhaps
fraction of flower here placing
an inch of air there) and

without breaking anything.

The entire poem is a simile; *like* in the first line of each stanza signals that fact. Spring is like a hand in a window, Cummings tells us. Similes are frequently used by poets, but this one strains English grammar because the hand referred to is a *perhaps hand. Perhaps* is an adverb by nature, and when an adverb modifies a noun, it normally follows that noun, as in *the folks upstairs, the party yesterday,* or *the air outside.* Cummings boldly puts *perhaps* in a favorite adjective position between the determiner *a* and the noun *hand.* Thus he produces *a perhaps hand,* which we might more grammatically describe as *a gentle hand* or *a skillful hand.* Cummings' distortion does not jar us unpleasantly because, as native speakers of English, we feel intuitively that *perhaps,* as he uses it, appropriately suggests the unpredictability of spring. As Frost writes, in "Two Tramps in Mud Time,"

. . . When the sun is out and the wind is still,
You're one month on in the middle of May.
But if you so much as dare to speak,
A cloud comes over the sunlit arch,
A wind comes off a frozen peak, 5
And you're two months back in the
middle of March.

When Cummings speaks of *a perhaps fraction of flower,* the grammar is strained even harder. In addition to being surprised by the strange pre-noun position of *perhaps,* we do not expect flowers to be fractioned. Still we "know" intuitively what Cummings means, especially when he parallels it with *an inch of air,* even though air is not usually measured by inches.

Cummings has some more fun with adverbs when he says, "to and fro moving New and Old things." Normal word order is *moving new and old things to and fro.* Yet here too his unusual word order does not block communication. Rather, the movability of adverbs enhances the changeability of spring.

The last line of the poem, *without breaking anything,* distorts English grammar more violently. Since it follows *and* in the preceding line, it clearly is the second half of a conjunction transform. In searching for its partner, we can strip out the parenthesis, which is grammatically separate from the rest of the stanza. Then we have left only:

spring is like a perhaps
Hand in a window . . . and
without breaking anything.

Although *in a window* and *without breaking anything* are both prepositional phrases, they are obviously not of equal grammatical weight. The former is a simple adverbial phrase of place, while *without breaking anything* is a transform from

spring is not breaking anything

Immediately the grammatical equality leaps out at us. Before transformation, the underlying sentence was indeed of equal grammatical weight with *spring is like a perhaps hand.* Thus we understand the subtle grammatical sensibility of E. E. Cummings. Although he distorts grammar more severely than does Frost, he is definitely writing grammatically acceptable English.

"Spring," by Gerard Manley Hopkins, is not visually startling, but its use of words is extremely unconventional.

Spring

Nothing is so beautiful as spring—
When weeds, in wheels, shoot long and lovely and lush;
Thrush's eggs look little low heavens, and thrush
Through the echoing timber does so rinse and wring
The ear, it strikes like lightnings to hear him sing; 5
The glassy peartree leaves and blooms, they brush
The descending blue; that blue is all in a rush
With richness; the racing lambs too have fair their fling.

Hopkins starts with a completely grammatical statement, *Nothing is so beautiful as spring.* In the second line, he lets the noun *weeds* select an unusual verb, *shoot,* to be its predicate and adds three surprising adjectives—*long, lovely, lush*—as complements for this verb, which usually is transitive, not linking. Into this line he also inserts the prepositional phrase, *in wheels,* which is grammatically surprising. In the third line, Hopkins omits a preposition, but we have no way of knowing which one. Therefore the line can mean *Thrush's eggs look like little low heavens* and *Thrush's eggs look at little low heavens.* Such is the grammatical force of the omission of a preposition. The second *thrush,* in line three, has as its predicate another strange pair of verbs—*rinse* and *wring*—with an even stranger direct object, *the ear.* Clothes, not ears, are usually rinsed and wrung. Human beings and machines, not birds, usually *rinse* and *wring.* Hopkins strains the grammar to the limit by describing the thrush's song as rinsing and wringing our ears. The rest of line five puts less tension on the grammar; completing the *so* in line four, Hopkins says:

> *to hear him* (the thrush) *sing strikes like lightnings.*

The semicolon at the end of line five is like a period marking the end of one grammatical part. The next part extends to the semicolon in the center of line seven. Between these semicolons Hopkins has created strange tensions. First, he separates his subject and predicate by a comma and then restates the subject with *they.* The comma breaks a standard English punctuation rule: Do not separate subject from predicate by a comma. The *they* adds a grammatically unnecessary word, repeating the subject. The meaning is:

> The leaves and blooms of the peartree brush the sky.

When we first read this line, *leaves* and *blooms* seem to be verbs rather than nouns. Hopkins brings us up short with the comma. The next word, *they,* establishes that *leaves* and *blooms* are nouns. Hopkins skillfully adds a surprising adjective, *glassy,* in front of the three nouns: *peartree, leaves,* and *blooms.* By doing so, he gets triple service from *glassy,* since it can and does modify all three nouns. Notice that the sky is called "the descending blue," again an unusual union of words, a slight strain on the grammar. Between the next set of semicolons the strain increases. We recognize *that blue* as the same sky, but for a sky to be *all in a rush with richness* is grammatically amazing, although intuitively satisfying. Spring skies are indeed full of rushing birds and their rich songs. The last eight words comprise a simple sentence with only one wandering word, *fair.* It can be an adjective thrown out of its normal position—*have their fair fling*—or a flat adverb—*have their fling fairly*—or a noun—*have their fling as at a fair.* Hopkins here again makes words work triply for him.

We have seen that grammatical English can range from completely conventional usage as shown in Browning's "Pippa's Song" to powerful distortions of grammatical patterns as shown in Hopkins' "Spring" without producing non-sentences. The poet can intensify his poem's power by exploiting the elasticity of English grammar.

Exercise one. Here is a set of word-groups punctuated like sentences. First, eliminate the non-sentences, the ones that would be used only by a foreign speaker of English. Then, for each sentence, make up a context into which it could fit sensibly. The more context you need, the less grammatical the sentence is. The sentence that requires the least context is the most grammatical. Try to rank the sentences on a scale from the most grammatical to the least grammatical, and explain your ranking. The important point of this exercise is your discussion of why you ranked the sentences as you did. There is no single correct ranking.

1. Is better careful to study.
2. Red and green terrify each other.
3. The molten ice flattered a shoe.
4. After marry her, he take her to Mexico.
5. Freedom is a breakfast food.
6. Golf plays John.
7. The boy shivers scissors.
8. John plays golf.
9. My friend didn't went and so I too do.
10. Coats are things women sit down too far up on.

Exercise two. Here are five versions of the first stanza of Lewis Carroll's "Jabberwocky." The first is Carroll's original. It is grammatical in spite of its nonsense words. The endings and function words of English are there to signal grammatical meanings like *noun, verb, adjective, subject,* and *predicate,* even though the words make little sense. The second version is ungrammatical in English; it is written in German.

The third version is less than fully grammatical. It has the right function words and the right parts of speech, but it has the wrong subclasses of the parts of speech. *Wire* and *sample* are verbs that do not work fully grammatically with the noun *knee.*

Nor are *cataracts* comfortably grammatical with the verb *weaseled. Cheese* and *wraths* form a less than fully grammatical modification structure.

The fourth version is more grammatical, and with a little effort we can imagine a context in which it might occur. This version is interesting because it stimulates the imagination to create a context for it. The final version is grammatical.

Write a paper explaining a situation or context into which the fourth version could fit easily and meaningfully. These papers should be compared to show that many different contexts are possible.

The Five Versions of "Jabberwocky"[1]

1. 'Twas brillig and the slithy toves
Did gyre and gimble in the wabe:
All mimsy were the borogoves,
And the mome raths outgrabe.

2. 'Swar wolkig, und der schlaue Dachs
Erwachte und schweifte durch das Land;
Sehr durstig war der kleine Lachs,
Und das Muscheltier verstand.

3. 'Twas baldish, and the slippery pacts
Did wire and sample in the knee;
All weaseled were the cataracts,
And the cheese wraths outflee.

4. 'Twas brittle, and the silly dopes
Did tire and grumble in the glade;
All mossy were the cantaloupes,
And the stone ducks decayed.

5. 'Twas chilly, and the sturdy lads
Did rush and bustle in their stride;
All ready were the launching pads
And the astronauts inside.

Exercise three. Here is group of five poems about young men dying in war. Observe how each poet stretches the grammar of English.

[1] Based on a version written by Robert B. Lees, University of Illinois.

In Flanders Fields

John McCrae

In Flanders fields the poppies blow
Between the crosses, row on row,
  That mark our place; and in the sky
  The larks, still bravely singing, fly,
Scarce heard amid the guns below. 5

We are the Dead. Short days ago
We lived, felt dawn, saw sunset glow,
  Loved and were loved; and now we lie
  In Flanders fields.

Take up our quarrel with the foe: 10
To you from failing hands we throw
  The torch; be yours to hold it high.
  If ye break faith with us who die
We shall not sleep, though poppies grow 15
  In Flanders field.

In this poem normal English has been distorted only slightly. In line 2, *row on row* grammatically goes with *crosses* but it can also work doubly with both *poppies* and *crosses.* In the second half of the first stanza, what similar slight distortion of normal word order do you observe? For what word does *scarce* substitute? What two parts of speech are interchanged?

Stanza two is also almost completely grammatical. The second sentence is divided by a semicolon. Why is the first part of this second sentence the less grammatical part? Note that we usually say "six days ago" or "a short time ago." What synonym would we probably use for the word *ye* in the third stanza?

Anthem for Doomed Youth

Wilfred Owen

What passing-bells for these who die as cattle?
  Only the monstrous anger of the guns.
  Only the stuttering rifles' rapid rattle
Can patter out their hasty orisons.
No mockeries for them from prayers or bells, 5
  Nor any voice of mourning save the choirs,—
The shrill, demented choirs of wailing shells;
  And bugles calling for them from sad shires.
What candles may be held to speed them all?
  Not in the hands of boys, but in their eyes 10

Shall shine the holy glimmers of good-byes.
  The pallor of girls' brows shall be their pall;
Their flowers the tenderness of patient minds,
And each slow dusk a drawing-down of blinds.

Defining a sentence as a noun phrase serving as subject plus a verb phrase serving as predicate, how many sentences can you count in this poem? (Include questions, and remember that a semicolon or a conjunction like "and" can divide two sentences as a period does.) We can fill in the missing verbs by supplying various forms of *be* either with or without the word *there*. For example, the question in line 1 can be completed:

What passing-bells *are there* for these who die as cattle?

(A *passing-bell* is a bell that tolls at a funeral.) How can you use the same device in lines 2 and 5? In line 6 what part of speech is *save* and what are its objects? In the second stanza, modals appear three times: *may* in line 9 and *shall* in lines 11 and 12. In lines 13 and 14 can you insert the proper modal and linking verb to fill out the sentence? In line 10, we would normally stress *boys*. Why must we shift this normal sentence accent to *hands*? In lines 10 and 11 nominal word order is twisted. Rearrange the words into a completely grammatical sentence.

An Irish Airman Foresees His Death

William Butler Yeats

I know that I shall meet my fate
Somewhere among the clouds above;
Those that I fight I do not hate,
Those that I guard I do not love;
My country is Kiltartan Cross, 5
My countrymen Kiltartan's poor,
No likely end could bring them loss
Or leave them happier than before.
Nor law, nor duty bade me fight,
Nor public men, nor cheering crowds, 10
A lonely impulse of delight
Drove to this tumult in the clouds;
I balanced all, brought all to mind,
The years to come seemed waste of breath,
A waste of breath the years behind 15
In balance with this life, this death.

The first two lines of the third poem make a completely grammatical statement, while lines 3 and 4 need some rearrangement. What irregularities do you detect in these two lines? Line 6 needs a linking verb. Which one and what form? Lines 9 and 10 have four instances of *nor*. In less poetical usage we would probably not use the verb *bade*. Rephrase the two lines, using *not*. In line 12 the direct object is omitted. Who was driven? In the last three lines the poet looks first into the future, then into the past, and finally at the present. Explain and rearrange line 15 into a fully grammatical sentence.

from La Guerre
E. E. Cummings

the bigness of cannon
is skillful,

but i have seen
death's clever enormous voice
which hides in a fragility 5
of poppies. . . .

i say that sometimes
on these long talkative animals
are laid fists of huger silence

I have seen all the silence 10
filled with vivid noiseless boys

at Roupy
i have seen
between barrages,

the night utter ripe unspeaking girls. 15

In "La Guerre" ("War") Cummings says that in war, silence speaks louder than cannons, "those long talkative animals." Count the words referring to silence and those referring to speech. Note that *utter* in the last line means "speak," though we usually think of words being uttered, not "ripe unspeaking girls."

The poem has strange capitalization and sometimes absent punctuation, but its word order is not radically distorted. For instance, the first two lines are an example of Basic Sentence Pattern 5 with one insertion, *of cannon*. In which line do you find an example of another pattern?

Although the word order is not radically distorted, Cummings has stretched the grammar by subclass distortion. For example, in *bigness . . . is skillful, skillful* is an unexpected predicate adjective to refer to the noun *bigness*. What other startling combinations does Cummings use?

from War Is Kind

Stephen Crane

Do not weep, maiden, for war is kind.
Because your lover threw wild hands toward the sky
And the affrighted steed ran on alone,
Do not weep.
War is kind. 5

Hoarse, booming drums of the regiment,
Little souls who thirst for fight,
These men were born to drill and die.
The unexplained glory flies above them,
Great is the battle-god, great, and his kingdom— 10
A field where a thousand corpses lie.

Do not weep, babe, for war is kind.
Because your father tumbled in the yellow trenches,
Raged at his breast, gulped and died,
Do not weep. 15
War is kind.

Swift blazing flag of the regiment,
Eagle with crest of red and gold,
These men were born to drill and die.
Point for them the virtue of slaughter, 20
Make plain to them the excellence of killing
And a field where a thousand corpses lie.

Mother whose heart hung humble as a button
On the bright splendid shroud of your son,
Do not weep. 25
War is kind.

In "War is Kind" the poet alternately addresses human beings and the trappings of war. First he speaks to the maiden, then to the drums of the regiment, then to the baby, then to the flag of the regiment, and finally to the mother. He tells the humans, "Do not weep, for war is kind"; he tells the drums and the flag, "These men were born to drill and die." These assertions contrast ironically, and this contrast is intensified by the linking of *war* and *kind* by *is*, once in the title and five times in the poem. Lines 20, 21, and 24 show other contradictory pairs of words. What are they? How are they linked?

When the poet begins to speak to the maiden and the baby, he uses a negative imperative transform with an adverbialization transform inserted into it. How does he change this structure at the end of the speeches to the maiden, the baby, and the mother?

Normal English word order is distorted only in line 10. Rearrange the words into normal word order, omitting one *great*. Line 9 is an example of Basic Sentence Pattern 1, with one adjectivalization transform, *unexplained*, inserted into it. After rearrangement, what two basic sentence patterns are exemplified by lines 10 and 11? What verb has been omitted at the end of line 10?

Lines 7 and 18 are appositives. One precedes its headword and the other follows its headword. Which is which? Line 2 and line 13 begin with the subordinator, *because*, which introduces adverbialization transforms. Count the verbs following each *because* to discover how many sentences underlie each adverbialization transform.

How do the insertions in lines 22 and 23 differ from those in lines 2–3 and 13–14?

These five poems have shown how different poets stretch English grammar for their own poetical purposes. The elasticity of the grammar gives them great freedom without danger of creating non-sentences. We do not reject their English, but instead we are challenged and charmed by it.

Exercise four. Here is one more poem to analyze, "You, Andrew Marvell," by Archibald MacLeish. Andrew Marvell was a seventeenth-century poet who wrote a famous poem about the swift passing of time, entitled "To His Coy Mistress." MacLeish probably had two lines from this poem especially in mind:

> But at my back I always hear
> Time's wingèd chariot hurrying near.

In "You, Andrew Marvell," the poet is stretched face down in the noon sun in the heart of the United States—Illinois, on the shore of Lake Michigan, MacLeish has said. The poet imagines night moving swiftly toward him from the other side of the earth. Ecbatan and Kermanshah are ancient cities of Persia, Baghdad is an ancient city of Iraq, and Palmyra is a ruined city northeast of Damascus in Syria. Westward from Persia, Iraq, Arabia, through Syria, Crete, Sicily, Spain, across Africa and the Atlantic Ocean, the night moves inexorably on.

The essence of the poem is relentless movement, communicated almost entirely by structure. There is no punctuation except the ellipsis points at the end, indicating an unfinished sentence. Our guide to its meaning lies in its grammar.

You, Andrew Marvell

Archibald MacLeish

And here face down beneath the sun
And here upon earth's noonward height
To feel the always coming on
The always rising of the night

To feel creep up the curving east 5
The earthly chill of dusk and slow
Upon those under lands the vast
And ever-climbing shadow grow

And strange at Ecbatan the trees
Take leaf by leaf the evening strange 10
The flooding dark about their knees
The mountains over Persia change

And now at Kermanshah the gate
Dark empty and the withered grass
And through the twilight now the late 15
Few travelers in the westward pass

And Baghdad darken and the bridge
Across the silent river gone
And through Arabia the edge
Of evening widen and steal on 20

And deepen on Palmyra's street
The wheel rut in the ruined stone
And Lebanon fade out and Crete
High through the clouds and overblown

And over Sicily the air 25
Still flashing with the landward gulls
And loom and slowly disappear
The sails above the shadowy hulls

And Spain go under and the shore
Of Africa the gilded sand 30
And evening vanish and no more
The low pale light across that land

Nor now the long light on the sea

And here face downward in the sun
To feel how swift how secretly 35
The shadow of the night comes on . . .

MacLeish uses *to feel* three times in the poem. In lines 3 and 4 it is followed by a pair of nominalization transforms:

. . . the . . . coming on [of the night]
. . . the . . . rising of the night

In lines 35 and 36 *to feel* is followed by a pair of adverbialization transforms. The first one is reduced to *how swift;* the second is not reduced:

. . . how secretly
The shadow of the night comes on . . .

In lines 5 through 34 *to feel* is followed by many insertions. These are linked together by *and's*. (Indeed, this poem is a set of conjunction transforms chained together by *and's.*) For example, look at lines 5 and 6:

[To feel] . . . creep up the curving east
The earthly chill of dusk . . .

which in normal English word order would be:

To feel the earthly chill of dusk creep up the curving east.

Here we see that when the sentence, *The earthly chill of dusk creeps up the curving east,* is transformed for insertion after *feel, creeps* becomes *creep.* In lines 6, 7, and 8 *grows* becomes *grow.* Rearranged into normal English word order, these lines say, "To feel the vast and ever-changing shadow grow slow[ly] upon those under[neath] lands."

Rearrange other insertions whose verbs are *take,* line 10; *change,* line 12; *pass,* line 16; *darken,* line 17; *fade out,* line 23; *go under,* line 29; and *vanish,* line 31.

In lines 20 and 21 three verbs have undergone conjunction transformation and work together in one insertion: *widen, steal on, deepen.* What is the subject of all three? What is the object of *deepen?* In line 27 two verbs appear: *loom* and *disappear.* What is their subject?

Slow in line 6 is a "flat" adverb. That is, it does not have the *-ly* ending we normally expect on it. It looks like an adjective but works like an adverb: *grow slow.* Find two more "flat" adverbs, one used twice. In lines 3 and 4 the use of *always* is intuitively satisfying to indicate the continuous and inevitable approach of night. However, this use of *always* is grammatically unusual. In what way does it strain the grammar of English? In line 3, why is *coming on* grammatically ambiguous?

In lines 15 and 16 we have *the late few travelers.* What is normal English word order for this phrase? Why does the poet make this switch? In line 2, why do you think MacLeish uses the strange word *noonward* instead of the ordinary word *noontime?* In lines 9 and 10 *strange* appears twice. What is the more normal grammatical form in both cases? Why is there no *and* between *evening* and the *strange* in line 10?

In line 16 can *pass* be read as a noun as well as a verb? Explain the word-play on *edge* and *steal* in lines 19 and 20. In line 21 *and deepen* goes backward and forward grammatically. How does this fact intensify the movement of the poem? Can *and loom and slowly disappear* in line 27 go with *gulls* as well as *sails?*

What effect does the poet create by chaining so many conjunction transforms together with *and*'s? Punctuate the poem intelligently and see where difficult (or impossible) decisions have to be made. Does punctuation ruin or improve the poem? Explain your answer.

CHAPTER FIVE

The Horizons of Grammar: Ambiguity

INTRODUCTION

The value of using language well cannot be questioned.

> Long experience with College Board examinations has shown that success in college, even for mathematics and science students, depends largely on "verbal skill"—ability to understand and use words. Therefore, extensive reading merely as verbal exercise . . . is an important part of college preparation.[1]

A comparison of the use of transformations by fourth-graders and twelfth-graders has revealed that fourth-graders of average intelligence can perform almost every transformation that twelfth-graders can.[2] However, in their writing, the fourth-graders use their ability much less than the twelfth-graders do. A fourth-grader probably would use an entire sentence to say what a twelfth-grader packs into a phrase or a word. Between the fourth and twelfth grades most students learn to write in a concise, adult style.

The result of applying grammar to reading and writing is more than practical improvement in these skills. When we read with understanding and write with clarity, we grow in ability to perceive our world. "Nothing is clear until we have put it into words," Bergson says, "for words are the only means of translating impressions to the intellect. Hence the immense help expression gives to vision, in clarifying it. The growth of the power of language is not merely a technical development, it implies a growth of vision."[3]

In this chapter and the next we will examine some of the problems we face as readers and writers, searching for solutions based on our understanding of English grammar. This chapter will consider ambiguity; the next chapter will consider variety.

---

1 *Reading List for College-Bound Students,* compiled by the Book List Committee of the Wisconsin Council of Teachers of English, n.d., p. 2.

2 See Kellogg W. Hunt, *Grammatical Structures Written at Three Grade Levels.* (Champaign, Illinois: National Council of Teachers of English, 1965)

3 Henri Bergson was a great French philosopher, who won the Nobel Prize for Literature in 1927. His statement is quoted by Professor Francis Christensen in "Notes toward a New Rhetoric," *College English* 25 (October 1963), p. 12.

AMBIGUITY

If someone asks, "What does the word *run* mean?" we must answer, "Its meaning depends on the context in which it is used." It could be a run in baseball, or in a stocking, or a synonym for *brook,* or a run of good luck. Standing alone the word is ambiguous; that is, it has more than one possible meaning. To make it clear we need more information about how it is being used. We need context—the frame of words that specifies which meaning is intended.

In speaking, we always add context by intonation and gesture, and we study our listener's face to see if he is understanding. In reading, context is supplied by the surrounding sentences. In writing, our sentences normally appear in context, which helps to prevent ambiguity. The wary writer is conscious of potential ambiguities and strives to avoid such traps. Poets deliberately use ambiguity of all kinds to add texture and depth to their writing.

Essentially ambiguities are of two kinds: lexical and grammatical. Each of these can be briefly illustrated by this set of ambiguous sentences, given here without context.

1. Would you feel put out if you were evicted?
2. The case is closed.

3. He owns a marvelous plant.
4. Racing greyhounds may be expensive.
5. The girls hated Joe's broiling.
6. Fatso brought the thin girl upstairs.

The first three sentences are lexically ambiguous. That is, some of the words in the sentences have more than one meaning in the dictionary. *Put out* can mean both "angry" and "evicted." *The case is closed* can mean either "The suitcase is shut" or "The court case is finished." In *He owns a marvelous plant,* the last word can mean "factory" or "flower."

The next three sentences are ambiguous because of their grammar. *Racing greyhounds may be expensive* can mean either "Greyhounds are expensive" or "Racing is expensive." The ambiguity is caused mainly by the *may,* one of the very few English modal auxiliaries, which do not use the *-s* suffix in the third person singular of the present tense. (The others are *can, will, shall,* and *must.*) *The girls hated Joe's broiling* can mean

The girls hated the way Joe did the broiling.
. . . the fact that Joe was doing the broiling.
. . . the fact that Joe was being broiled.
. . . the way that Joe was being broiled.

The ambiguity arises because *broil* can be either a transitive or an intransitive verb. In a sentence like *Joe will broil the steak, broil* is a transitive verb with its direct object, *the steak.* On the other hand, in a sentence like *The steak will broil over the embers, broil* is an intransitive verb because it lacks a direct object, being completed only by an adverbial phrase, *over the embers.* The sentence, *Fatso brought the thin girl upstairs,* can mean:

The thin girl was downstairs and Fatso brought her upstairs.
Fatso brought the thin girl who lived upstairs (to the party).

The problem here is *upstairs,* which can modify either *girl* or *brought.*

Sometimes we find both lexical and grammatical ambiguity present in a sentence. Here is an example:

Poles are used to fish.

The word *poles* is lexically ambiguous, although only in writing. In speech *used to* is pronounced differently depending on the meaning intended, but in writing, *Poles* can be interpreted as either "Polish people" or "fishing poles." In the first interpretation *used to* is equivalent to *accustomed to* and *fish* is a noun. (Polish people are used to [eating] fish.) In the second interpretation, the entire sentence is a passive transform of

Someone} uses poles to fish.

Thus we have grammatical ambiguity in addition to lexical ambiguity.

In the sentence, *The leaves were piled up by the truck,* the preposition *by* can be synonymous with *near,* or it can signal the performer in a passive transform of the basic sentence, *The truck piled up the leaves.* As native speakers of English, we know that both interpretations are possible. The context surrounding the sentence will identify which interpretation is proper.

Exercise one. Study the following ambiguous sentences, and explain their ambiguities by giving two or more paraphrases of them. Name the kind of ambiguities, grammatical or lexical—or both—that appear in each sentence.

1. The art class admires Mary's modeling.
2. He saw the purple people eaters.
3. Junior knew nicer men than Dad.
4. They looked higher than the Golden Gate Bridge.
5. The referee seemed unfair to Stilts Jackson.
6. Can you put up with vinegar?
7. Mary told Carolyn about herself.
8. The senators got through the opening of the project.
9. Algernon didn't get the connection and missed the fun.
10. Confusing orders can be disastrous.

LEXICAL AMBIGUITY

Lexical ambiguity usually can be avoided by adding context. For example, *ring* is lexically ambiguous in the sentence, *There was a ring around it.* If we change *it* to *the bathtub,* this additional context removes the ambiguity. In the sentence, *He caught the fly, fly* is lexically ambiguous. If we add *for the third out,* we make clear that the fly is not an insect but part of a baseball game.

© United Feature Syndicate, Inc. 1956

Time can complicate lexical ambiguity. For example, in his poem, "The Lotos-Eaters," Tennyson describes waterfalls as "slow dropping veils of thinnest lawn." The modern meaning of *lawn* does not fit. Clearly, the meaning must have changed since Tennyson's day. A dictionary tells us that when Tennyson wrote "The Lotos-Eaters" (1832), *lawn* meant "filmy cloth used for ladies' summer dresses." Our knowledge of possible lexical ambiguity thus can help us read literature more intelligently. All the italicized words in the following excerpts have unexpected meanings.

> . . . I only hear
> Its melancholy, long, withdrawing roar,

Retreating, to the breath
Of the night-wind, down the vast edges drear
And naked *shingles* of the world *(small beach stones)*

From "Dover Beach"
by Matthew Arnold, 1867.

The leading *files* of the regiment had nearly *(ranks)*
attained the brow of the steep hill we have
mentioned, when two or three horsemen,
speedily *discovered* to be a part of their own *(revealed)*
advanced guard, who had acted as a patrol,
appeared returning at full gallop, their horses
much *blown*, and the men apparently in a dis- *(winded)*
ordered flight. They were followed *upon the*
spur by five or six riders, well armed with *(at full speed)*
sword and pistol, who halted upon the top of
the hill, on observing the approach of the Life-
Guards. One or two who had carbines dis-
mounted, and, taking a leisurely and deliberate
aim at the foremost rank of the regiment, dis-
charged their *pieces*, by which two troopers *(weapons)*
were wounded, one severely. . . .

From *Old Mortality*
by Sir Walter Scott, 1816.

But before they had even approached it they
heard the bull scampering through the pond
without, and in a second he dashed into the *(outside)*
barn, knocking down the *hurdle-stake* in pass- *(fence pole)*
ing; the heavy door slammed behind him; and
all three were imprisoned in the barn together.
The *mistaken* creature saw them, and stalked *(wrongly caught)*
towards the end of the barn into which they
had fled. The girls *doubled* so adroitly that *(turned back on their course)*
their pursuer was against the wall when the
fugitives were already half way to the other
end. . . .

From *The Mayor of Casterbridge*
by Thomas Hardy, 1886.

His spear, a *bent* both stiff and strong *(blade of grass)*
And well-near of two inches long;
The *pile* was of a horse-flea's tongue *(point)*
Whose sharpness naught reversed.

From "Nymphidia"
by Michael Drayton, 1627.

I sigh the lack of many a thing I sought
And with old woes new wail my *dear* time's waste. *(precious)*

From "Sonnet 30"
by William Shakespeare, 1609.

Puns are the result of an author's deliberate use of a word in two senses at once. Charles Lamb said, "[A pun] is a pistol let off at the ear; not a feather to tickle the intellect." But many authors have used puns for their artistic purposes, and to good effect.

Here are a few puns by a modern writer, Richard Armour, commenting on "Captains of Industry" in *It All Started with Columbus.*

Andrew Carnegie

Carnegie made his money in steel. Although he was a mild, soft-spoken man, his steel had quite a temper. . . .
Carnegie was so well known for his philanthropy that he became an Institution.

John D. Rockefeller

Rockefeller made his money in oil, which he discovered at the bottom of wells. Oil was crude in those days, but so was Rockefeller. Now both are considered quite refined. . . .
He was admired for his skill in a game called Monopoly, which was an effective way of eliminating competitors and establishing a single standard, such as Standard Oil.

J. P. Morgan

Morgan, who was a direct sort of person, made his money in money. He lived in an airy mansion, full of bank drafts, called the House of Morgan. . . .
An ingenious invention of Morgan's was a means of floating government loans which made it possible to send large sums of money across the Atlantic without using ships. He became immensely wealthy because of his financial interests which were around eight or ten per cent.

John Dryden's (1631–1700) pun in "Death of Amyntas" demonstrates that not all puns are as jarring as a pistol shot.[4]

[4] This example and the two following it are drawn from William Empson's *Seven Types of Ambiguity* (Meridian Books edition) pp. 122-124.

but soon he found
The Welkin pitched with sullen Clouds around,
An Eastern Wind, and Dew upon the ground.

Welkin means "sky," and thus *pitched* means both "blackened as with pitch by the thunderclouds" and "pitched like a tent." In "Rival Ladies" Dryden uses the same pun:

O call that Night again;
Pitch her with all her Darkness round; then set me
In some far Desert, hemm'd with Mountain Wolves
To howl about me.

In "The Vanity of Human Wishes" Dr. Samuel Johnson (1709–1784) puns on the words *heady* and *will.*

The watchful guests still hint the last offence,
The daughter's petulance, the son's expense;
Improve his heady rage with treacherous skill,
And mould his passions till they make his will.

Heady means both that the father was the head of the family and that his anger soon came to a head. *Will* means both the father's "last will and testament" and his "wish" or "desire." Thomas Hood (1799–1845) wrote:

And even the stable-boy will find
This life no stable thing.

In these lines Hood used *stable* as a noun referring to the place where cattle are housed, and also as an adjective meaning "firm."

John Milton (1608–1674) wrote:

at one bound
High overleaps all bounds.

Here *bound* is used in the sense of "a leap" and "a boundary."

Shakespeare (1564–1616), whose works contain many puns, has Mark Anthony say in *Julius Caesar:*

O world, thou wast the forest to this hart
And this indeed, O world, the heart of thee—

The pun involves two different words—*hart* and *heart*—that are pronounced the same. Margaret Schlauch lists these puns from the opening pages of James Joyce's (1882–1941) *Finnegans Wake:*[5]

[5] In "Language and Poetic Creation," from *The Gift of Tongues* (New York: The Viking Press, 1942).

doublin Dublin, doublin (doubling)
retaled retailed, re-taled (*i.e.*, told again)
wills wills (noun) and wills (verb, opposite to "won'ts")
wan wan, one
lean on lean on, lien on

These two lines from Gerard Manley Hopkins' (1844–1889) "The Windhover" have stimulated many critics to write about the interpretation of *buckle:*

> Brute beauty and valour and act, oh, air, pride, plume here
> Buckle!

Buckle can mean "fasten, enclose, limit, set to work, bend completely, join, grapple, engage with an adversary, cringe, submit, marry." All work here.

Exercise one. Add enough context to remove the lexical ambiguities in these sentences. Example:

Look at the table. (*Table* is ambiguous.)
Look at the table of contents in this book. (Added context removes the lexical ambiguity.)

1. Bill wore a light sweater to the rehearsal.
2. They had a good time in the drivers' pool.
3. The tie was amazing.
4. Ellie took the car to the shop.
5. The children couldn't influence his will.
6. Bill fell from a tree next to the bank.
7. He took the cue and began to play.
8. The girls can wear their skirts longer.
9. Jeremy moved one foot.
10. Doug cut across the diamond.
11. The doctor's wife drove him to the asylum.
12. Sackett ran after Morris.

Exercise two. Add other context to reveal a second meaning in the sentences of Exercise 1.

Exercise three. Select three words from the following list and write an ambiguous sentence for each. Then have a classmate remove the ambiguity by adding more context.

bag (as a noun) line (as a noun)
cover (as a verb) raise (as a verb)

deep (as an adjective)	high (as an adjective)
pipe (as a noun)	drift (as a noun)
pan (as a verb)	cut (as a verb)
cool (as an adjective)	bright (as an adjective)
soldier (as a verb)	band (as a noun)
rich (as an adjective)	cross (as a verb)
pool (as a noun)	dumb (as an adjective)

Exercise four. Here are five jokes from Bennett Cerf's *The Laugh's on Me* that depend for their humor on a pun. Explain the pun by stating the two lexical meanings of words that are lexically ambiguous.

"Golly," exclaimed a husband, "this liniment makes my shoulders smart." Suggested his wife, "Why not rub some on your head."

Consider the postage stamp. Its usefulness consists in the ability to stick to one thing till it gets there.

The frugal wife who discovered a foolproof way to hold bills down. She switched to a heavier paperweight.

Emily Kimbrough was about to deliver a lecture recently when a workman appeared on the stage, waving a screwdriver and beckoning the chairlady. There followed a hasty conference, whereupon the chairlady brushed past Miss Kimbrough and told the standing-room audience, "I'm sorry to say there will be a slight delay. Word has just been given me that there is a screw loose in our speaker."

A six-foot beanpole in the Middle West made the all-collegiate basketball honor roll but floundered desperately in the classroom. "My boy won his fourth letter this winter," boasted his coach. "Humpf," snorted his faculty adviser, "I'll bet you had to read it to him."

Exercise five. Here is a Tom Swifty joke that is a wonderful collection of puns.

"And then, still with no clothes on, I ran through the screen door again, again forgetting to open it," wired Tom, barely restraining himself.

Here are three more samples:

"The horse has just stopped," snorted Tom woefully.
"That sweater is about her size," estimated Tom figuratively.

"The troops can't march any farther," commanded Tom haltingly.

Do you know any other Tom Swifty jokes, or can you make up some?

Exercise six. The following sentences seem foolish because one word in each is used in an archaic or obsolete meaning. In other words, they are ambiguous because the word has a modern meaning different from its older meaning. By tracking down the old meaning of each italicized word, prove that the sentences are sensible if these words are understood in their old meaning. Use several dictionaries to find the old meanings.

1. He snared the lion by means of a *necklace.*
2. Emma left the store carrying her empty *budget.*
3. Franklin was so *nice* that he didn't even know how to spell his name.
4. The *banquet* is uncomfortable and seats only one person.
5. The moths *fretted* the mink coat.
6. The *camera* was large enough to house the whole family.

GRAMMATICAL AMBIGUITY

Words Shift Part of Speech

Grammatical ambiguity often is caused by a word's occurrence as more than one part of speech. For instance, the word *round* can be:

an adjective: Santa Claus has a *round* stomach.

a verb: Their racing cars always *round* that corner on two wheels.

a noun: Doctor Kildare played a snappy *round* of golf yesterday.

an adverb: The maelstrom whirled *round* and *round.*

a preposition: Dracula peered *round* the dungeon.

In the following lines from Matthew Arnold's "Dover Beach," our understanding of the poem depends on our interpretation of the part of speech represented by *round.*

The Sea of Faith
Was once, too, at the full, and round earth's shore
Lay like the folds of a bright girdle furled.

The choice lies between *round* as an adjective—*round* earth—or *round* as a preposition equivalent to *around—(a)round* the earth's shore. *At the full* means "at full (or high) tide." That is, *full* can be a noun; it does not have to be an adjective and parallel with *round* as an adjective. If we do not read *round* as a preposition, there is no subject for the verb *lay.* With the prepositional reading, *The Sea of Faith* is clearly the subject of the two verbs, *was* and *lay.* Rearranged into normal English word order, the lines read "The Sea of Faith was once, too, at high tide and lay furled around the earth's shore like the folds of a bright sash."

An interesting problem results from Arnold's use of *girdle.* Many modern readers, reacting to the strong present-day connotations of the word, find it out of place even though they are aware of its intended meaning.

One of our main aids in deciding a word's part of speech is alertness to twists of normal word order. As in the poem above, when we rearrange the words into normal word order, the parts of speech become clear. Here are some typical kinds of rearrangements we often must make.[6]

---

[6] The following quotations are from Seymour B. Chatman's "Linguistics and Teaching Introductory Literature," *Language Learning* VIII (1956-1957) pp. 3-10, reprinted in *Readings in Applied English Linguistics,* 2nd ed. (New York: Appleton-Century-Crofts, 1964) Harold B. Allen, ed., p. 505.

Poetic:

Subject	*Object*	*Verb*
Bright Thames	thy brightest beauties	yield

Normal:

Subject	*Verb*	*Object*
Bright Thames	yield	thy brightest beauties

Poetic:

Object	*Subject*	*Verb*
no credit	doubting wits	may give

Normal:

Subject	*Verb*	*Object*
doubting wits	may give	no credit

Poetic:

Object	*Verb*	*Subject*
no mate	hath	he

Normal:

Subject	*Verb*	*Object*
he	hath	no mate

Exercise one. In the following sentences the italicized word causes grammatical ambiguity because it can belong to two parts of speech. In each case, identify the two parts of speech and then rewrite each sentence in two ways to test your analysis. Example:

> The *game* referee grabbed the blazing wastebasket.

Game can be either a noun or an adjective. As a noun:

> The referee in control of the game grabbed the blazing wastebasket.

As an adjective:

> The brave referee grabbed the blazing wastebasket.

1. J. Farrell Bledsoe is a *criminal* lawyer.
2. The Dalmatian looked *faster* than the beagle.
3. The rattlesnake looked as *long* as the cobra.
4. Dr. Johnson looked *over* Tony's head.
5. The organization wants to help *beat* musicians.
6. In this game *even* numbers work.

Exercise two. Some sentences are ambiguous only in writing, not in speaking. How many of the sentences in Exercise 1 are unambiguous when spoken aloud? Say each sentence with two different intonation patterns. On the other hand, some sentences are ambiguous in speaking but not in writing. Examples are:

> The plane/plain is burning.
> He rode/rowed for a long time.
> He looked for the tea/tee.

What signaling system of writing is lacking in speaking?

© United Feature Syndicate, Inc. 1953

Exercise three. We saw in the second chapter that omitting auxiliaries and determiners can easily cause ambiguity in telegrams and headlines. Here are four more headlines where the ambiguity is caused by words shifting part of speech. Identify the shifting words in each and name the parts of speech which are possible.

1. VAN GOGH DRAWS WELL
2. GEORGIA BRANDS RIGHT
3. MEAN TO CONTINUE BOMBINGS JOHNSON SAYS
4. BIOLOGY DEPARTMENT STUDIES OUTDOORS

Transformations Hide Structure

Sentences may be grammatically ambiguous in another way. When a sentence is transformed and inserted into a receiver, this transformation often hides the structure of the basic sentence. For example, the two prepositional phrases in the following sentences seem to have the same structure, whereas actually the basic sentences underlying them are quite different.

1. Willy shot the kid in the raincoat.
2. Willy shot the kid in the arm.

The two prepositional phrases come from the basic sentences below the receiver.

Receiver
Willy shot the kid.

1. The kid was in the raincoat.
2. The kid had an arm.
   The shot was in the arm.

In the derived sentence, *He seems grateful to me,* we cannot know whether underlying it is the basic sentence, *He is grateful to me,* or the derived sentence that has been produced from the receiver *I think* {Something} plus the nominal insert, *that he seems grateful.* Its derivational history is hidden by transformation. Ambiguity is the result.

Now consider this set of sentences.

1. Flashing signals can be exciting.
2. Duncan burned a picture of the girl that had upset his emotions.
3. He called his sister a waitress.

What do we know about the possible underlying sentences of each insert?

In sentence 1, *flashing* is the insert. Since *flash* can be either a transitive or an intransitive verb, the underlying basic sentences can be either

1. Signals flash.

or

2. {Someone} flashes signals.

Therefore the derived sentence can be interpreted either as *Signals that flash can be exciting,* or *The flashing of signals can be exciting.* In this case, *that flash* is a relative clause and *the flashing of signals* is a gerund, two different types of inserts.

In sentence 2, *that had upset his emotions* is a relative clause. Without context, ambiguity arises because, although the receiver is, clearly, *Duncan burned a picture of the girl,* the inserts can come from the basic sentence:

The picture had upset his emotions

or

The girl had upset his emotions.

In our writing, this kind of ambiguous derived sentence is a constant menace. In such sentences two nouns are present, and either of them could be modified by the relative clause.

In sentence 3, we cannot be sure of the receiver. It can be either *He called his sister,* or *He called a waitress.* In the first case, the basic sentence underlying the insert is *His sister is a waitress.* In the second case, it is *The waitress is for his sister.* The same ambiguity underlies the old joke in which one person says to another: "Call me a cab," and receives the answer, "O.K., you're a cab."

Understanding that transformations hide structure is helpful in avoiding or correcting *danglers.* Danglers are transforms inserted into receivers. The problem is that the subject of the dangler and the subject of the receiver are different when they should be the same. This fault creates ambiguous, often humorous, statements. Here are three sentences with danglers:

Riding down the road, the signs flash past.
Broken by illness, his death was a blessing.
Dumb with surprise, the news came as a great shock.

Riding down the road, the signs flash past sounds as if the signs are riding down the road when we know that really a person is riding. One way to identify a dangler is to place it after the subject of the receiver and make the dangler's verb the main verb.

The signs ride down the road.
His death was broken by illness.
The news was dumb with surprise.

In *Riding down the road, the signs flash past,* the two underlying basic sentences are

1. The signs flash past.
2. {Someone} is riding down the road.

Who can substitute for *someone* in sentence 2 and produce the insert, . . . *who is riding down the road.* The relative clause reduces to . . . *riding down the road.* If we stop here, we have a dangler because there is no overlap. A third basic sentence can supply the necessary overlap:

3. {Someone} sees the signs.

He can substitute for *someone* in sentence 3. *Signs* now overlaps *signs* in sentence 1: *The signs flash past. Which* can substitute for this *signs: . . . which flash past.* Now we can subtract the *which* and have a sentence with no dangler:

Riding down the road, he sees the signs flash past.

Another way to correct a dangler is by an adverbialization transformation.

As he is riding down the road, the signs flash past.

In adverbialization, no overlap is required. The subject of each sentence can be different, and the relationship between them is shown by the subordinator. Happily, any sentence can be adverbialized.

In *Broken by illness, his death was a blessing,* the underlying sentence of the dangler is *He was broken by illness,* a passive transform of *Illness broke him.* The dangler can be removed by adverbialization:

Because he was broken by illness, his death was a blessing.

The last dangler, *Dumb with surprise,* has as its underlying sentence:

He was dumb with surprise.

To remove the dangler we can use a conjunction transformation:

He was dumb with surprise, and the news came as a great shock.

Exercise four. In each of these grammatically ambiguous sentences explain what has been concealed by transformation. Then add enough context to remove the ambiguity.

1. He worries about promising students.
2. They asked him about racing cars.
3. The police must stop fighting after midnight.
4. Entertaining relatives can be fun.
5. It's too hot to eat. (Try *the dog, the soup,* and *the weather* as substitutions for *it.*)
6. They laughed at Jim's pushing.
7. Preston interviewed the man with the dog that was sick.
8. He found him a jackass.

Exercise five. Sometimes speech can furnish us enough context to remove grammatical ambiguity. Say these ambiguous sentences aloud, giving them two intonation patterns to reveal two different underlying basic sentences. Then write two unambiguous sentences expressing these two interpretations. Example:

Betty went to the little girls school.
Betty went to the school for little girls.
Betty went to the little school for girls.

The absence of an apostrophe in *girls* (the little girl's school) removes a third interpretation that would be possible in speech:

Betty went to the school where the little girl goes.

1. She showed the baby pictures.
2. People who study often get good marks.
3. Eating apples will be healthful.
4. Her father gave her more than enough money.
5. Mrs. Neilson was a Danish pastry cook.

Exercise six. Write the underlying sentence for each dangler. Then rewrite the sentence to eliminate the dangler, which is a source of grammatical ambiguity.

1. To avoid being tied up in traffic, the grandstands emptied early in the last quarter.
2. Confessing his guilt, the crime was solved.
3. Stuffed with pizza and coke, the party went merrily on.
4. Laid low by a common cold, the hospital was the best place for him.

THE POWER OF CONTEXT

Context is extremely powerful. People in the grip of one context resist a different interpretation and seem almost oblivious of ambiguity. For instance, the sentence, *Flying planes can be dangerous,* is ambiguous. However, we can condition one group by telling them about the terrible air crashes in Elizabeth, New Jersey, and how the residents petitioned to have the airport relocated farther away from their homes. This group of people will interpret *Flying planes can be dangerous* as *Planes that are flying are dangerous; those on the ground are not.* On the other hand, a second group of people can be conditioned by describing the dangerous life of the Air Force pilot, his long and arduous training, his danger of crashing or having to parachute to safety. This group of people will interpret *Flying planes can be dangerous* as *Flying planes is dangerous.* Each group will tend to think that the other interpretation is surprising or unlikely.

Computers behave in quite unhuman ways in interpreting ambiguous sentences. Jane J. Robinson, researcher at RAND Corporation in California, tells of giving this sentence to a computer to analyze:

I saw the man with the telescope in the park.

The computer produced the four expected analyses:

1. I was in the park and I had a telescope with which I saw the man.
2. I was in the park and the man had a telescope when I saw him.
3. I was in the park that had a telescope with which I saw the man.
4. The man was with the telescope that was in the park when I saw him.[7]

However, four unexpected interpretations appeared also. Unlike the human researchers, the computer was not in the grip of one context. Therefore it found not only grammatical ambiguity but lexical as well. The computer read *saw* not only as the past tense

[7] Two other interpretations are possible, but the computer had not been programmed to produce these: *The man was in the park and he had a telescope when I saw him;* and *I had a telescope and the man was in the park when I saw him.* For a full description of Jane Robinson's research see *Automatic Parsing and Fact Retrieval: A Comment on Grammar, Paraphrase, and Meaning* (Memorandum RM-4005-PR) (Santa Monica, California: The RAND Corporation, 1964).

of *see,* but also as the present tense of *saw* meaning "to cut with a saw." Certainly a telescope is a very dull cutting tool. Context prevents us from making this absurd interpretation, but the computer was logically using the information stored in its memory that English has a transitive verb *saw* as well as a transitive verb *see.*

Exercise one. Select one of the following potentially ambiguous inserts, and place it in a receiver that permits two interpretations. To test the power of context, write a background description for one interpretation. Read your description to two of your classmates. Then ask them to explain the other possible interpretation.

burning wires	rolling stones	exciting revolutions
teasing girls	boiling liquids	charming snakes

Exercise two. This poem by Gerard Manley Hopkins presents some interesting problems relating to ambiguity.

Spring and Fall:
to a young child

Márgarét, are you gríeving
Over Goldengrove unleaving?
Leáves, líke the things of man, you
With your fresh thoughts care for, can you?
Ah! ás the heart grows older 5
It will come to such sights colder
By and by, nor spare a sigh
Though worlds of wanwood leafmeal lie;
And yet you wíll weep and know why.
Now no matter, child, the name: 10
Sórrow's spríngs áre the same.
Nor mouth had, no nor mind, expressed
What heart heard of, ghost guessed:
It ís the blight man was born for,
It is Margaret you mourn for. 15

In line 2 *Goldengrove unleaving* means "a grove of trees losing its golden-yellow leaves." In line 8 Hopkins invents two new words—*wanwood* and *leafmeal.* In *wanwood, wan* can mean "pale, lusterless, languid, dark and dusky." Combined with *wood* it carries all these possible interpretations. *Leafmeal* suggests *piecemeal* and also the rotting of fallen leaves into mealy pieces. In line 13 *ghost* can mean "spirit," as in *Holy Ghost.* In line 11, what are the interpretations *springs* can have?

Exercise three. In the following excerpt from "Mr. K*A*P*L*A*N and Shakespeare," Leonard Q. Ross depicts Mr. Kaplan as a man in the grip of a context. Mr. Kaplan is a student in Mr. Parkhill's night class for adults learning to speak English. Mr. Parkhill has asked the class to use this famous soliloquy from Shakespeare's *Macbeth* as a topic for a short speech, telling what thoughts and ideas it brings to mind.

> To-morrow, and to-morrow, and to-morrow,
> Creeps in this petty pace from day to day
> To the last syllable of recorded time,
> And all our yesterdays have lighted fools
> The way to dusty death. Out, out, brief candle!
> Life's but a walking shadow, a poor player
> That struts and frets his hour upon the stage
> And then is heard no more: it is a tale
> Told by an idiot, full of sound and fury,
> Signifying nothing.

Finally Mr. Kaplan's turn comes. Mr. Parkhill says, "Mr. Kaplan, will *you* speak next?"

> Mr. Kaplan's face broke into a glow; his smile was like a rainbow. "Soitinly," he said, walking to the front of the room. Never had he seemed so dignified, so eager, so conscious of a great destiny.
>
> "Er—Mr. Kaplan," added Mr. Parkhill, suddenly aware of the possibilities which the situation (Kaplan on Shakespeare) involved: "Speak *carefully.*"
>
> "*Spacially* careful vill I be," Mr. Kaplan reassured him. He cleared his throat, adjusted his tie, and began: "Ladies an' gantleman, you hoid all kinds minninks abot dis piece poyetry, an'—"
>
> "*Po*etry."
>
> "—abot dis piece *po*etry. But to me is a difference minnink altogadder. Ve mus' tink abot Julius Scissor an' how *he* falt!"
>
> Mr. Parkhill moved nervously, puzzled.
>
> "In dese exact voids is Julius Scissor sayink—"
>
> "Er—Mr. Kaplan," said Mr. Parkhill once he grasped the full import of Mr. Kaplan's error. "The passage is from 'Macbeth.'"
>
> Mr. Kaplan looked at Mr. Parkhill with injured surprise. "*Not* fromm 'Julius Scissor'?" There was pain in his voice.
>
> "No. And it's—er—'Julius *Cae*sar.'"
>
> Mr. Kaplan waited until the last echo of the name had permeated his soul. "Podden me, Mr. Pockheel. Isn't '*see*zor' vat you cottink somting op mit?"

"That," said Mr. Parkhill quickly, "is 'scissor.' You have used 'Caesar' for 'scissor' and 'scissor' for 'Caesar.' "

Mr. Kaplan nodded, marvelling at his own virtuosity.

"But go on with your speech, please." Mr. Parkhill, to tell the truth, felt a little guilty that he had not announced at the very beginning that the passage was from "Macbeth." "Tell us *why* you thought the lines were from 'Julius Caesar.' "

"Vell," said Mr. Kaplan to the class, his smile assuming its normal serenity. "I vas positif, becawss I can *see* de whole ting." He paused, debating how to explain this cryptic remark. Then his eyes filled with a strange enchantment. "I see de whole scinn. It's in a tant, on de night bafore dey makink Julius de Kink fromm Rome. So he is axcited an' ken't slip. He is layink in bad, tinking: 'Tomorrow an' tomorrow an' tomorrow. How slow dey movink! Almost cripps! Soch a pity de pace!' "

Before Mr. Parkhill could explain that "petty pace" did not mean "Soch a pity de pace!" Mr. Kaplan had soared on.

"De days go slow, fromm day to day, like leetle tsyllables on phonograph racords fromm time."

Anxiety and bewilderment invaded Mr. Parkhill's eyes.

" 'An' vat abot yestidday?' tinks Julius Scissor. Ha! 'All our yestiddays are only makink a good light for fools to die in de dost!' "

" 'Dusty death' doesn't mean—" There was no interrupting Mr. Kaplan.

"An' Julius Scissor is so tired, an' he vants to fallink aslip. So he hollers, mit fillink, 'Go ot! Go ot! Short candle!' So it goes ot."

Mr. Kaplan's voice dropped to a whisper. "But he ken't slip. Now is bodderink him de idea fromm life. 'Vat is de life altogadder?' tinks Julius Scissor. An' he gives enswer, de pot I like de bast. 'Life is like a bum actor, strottink an' hollerink arond de stage for only vun hour bafore he's kicked ot. Life is a tale told by idjots, dat's all, full of fonny sonds an' phooey!' "

Mr. Parkhill could be silent no longer. " 'Full of sound and fury!' " he cried desperately. But inspiration, like an irresistible force, swept Mr. Kaplan on.

" 'Life is monkey business! It don' minn a ting. It signifies nottink!' An' den Julius Scissor closes his ice fest—" Mr. Kaplan demonstrated the Consul's exact ocular process in closing his "ice"—"—an' falls dad!"

The class was hushed as Mr. Kaplan stopped. In the silence, a tribute to the fertility of Mr. Kaplan's imagination and the power of his oratory, Mr. Kaplan went to his seat. But just before he sat down, as if adding a postscript, he sighed: "Dat vas mine idea. But ufcawss is all wronk, becawss Mr. Pockheel said de voids ain't abot Julius Scissor altogadder. It's all abot an Irishman by de name Macbat."

Then Mr. Kaplan sat down.

From *The Education of H*y*m*a*n K*a*p*l*a*n*
by Leonard Q. Ross.

Exercise four. The following groups of sentences show three ways to express approximately the same idea. One sentence in each group is not ambiguous.

1. (*a*) Coach Crosby stated in the auditorium that he condemned fighting.
   (*b*) Coach Crosby stated that he condemned fighting in the auditorium.
   (*c*) Coach Crosby stated that in the auditorium he condemned fighting.

In this group, sentence *a* is unambiguous. Placing the prepositional phrase, *in the auditorium,* immediately after *stated* clearly shows that this phrase modifies that verb and not *fighting.* The other two sentences seem to say that Crosby does not want any fights in the auditorium.

2. (*a*) Driving slowly through the empty streets, many fieldstone and redwood houses were seen.
   (*b*) Driving slowly through the empty streets, they saw many fieldstone and redwood houses.
   (*c*) Driving slowly through the empty streets, their eyes were met by many fieldstone and redwood houses.

In this group, only sentence *b* lacks a dangler. *They* is the subject of both the insert and the receiver. In the other two sentences, it sounds as if either the houses or the eyes are driving slowly through the empty streets.

3. (*a*) Either someone had hit her in the eye or she was wearing a lot of makeup.
   (*b*) Someone had hit her either in the eye or she was wearing a lot of makeup.
   (*c*) Someone had either hit her in the eye or she was wearing a lot of makeup.

Here the fault is in parallelism. The two sentences, *Someone hit her in the eye* and *She was wearing a lot of makeup,* are joined by a conjunction transformation. *Either* and *or* work together to join the two sentences and, by standing before them, signal that the sentences are parallel. If we insert *either* into one of the sentences, we lose parallelism. Therefore sentence *a* shows the proper way to perform the conjunction transformation. Other pairs that can work like *either . . . or* are *neither . . . nor,* and *not only . . . but also.* These conjunctions are called *correlatives.*

4. (*a*) Agnes made a scene, and the argument was won by her.
   (*b*) Agnes made a scene and won the argument.
   (*c*) A scene was made and Agnes won the argument.

This group involves a conjunction transformation. The two basic sentences combined are *Agnes made a scene* and *Agnes won the argument.* The subjects overlap, and in sentence *b* this overlapping is used to create a smooth sentence. Each half of sentence *a* and sentence *c* has a different subject. Half of each is a basic sentence, and half is a passive transform.

5. (*a*) The opportunity to be chosen to speak is useful in helping one to acquire self-confidence.
   (*b*) The opportunity to speak is useful in helping one to acquire self-confidence.
   (*c*) The opportunity to speak helps one to acquire self-confidence.

Here the problem is one of too much inserting, resulting in excessive wordiness. Sentence *c* is the shortest and the most effective sentence.

6. (*a*) To score is when a player puts the ball through the basket.
   (*b*) Scoring is owing to putting the ball through the basket.
   (*c*) To score is to put the ball through the basket.

Here the problem involves both parallelism and nominal inserts. *Is* stands like an equals sign between the two parts of each sentence. The two infinitives in sentence *c* show this grammatical equality in a parallel fashion. *To score* and *to put* are equal grammatically. Sentence *b* has the gerunds *scoring* and *owing* on each side of *is,* but the parallel ideas are *scoring* and *putting.* Sentence *a* says that a gerund nominal, *scoring,* equals an adverbial of time, *when a player puts the ball through the basket.* Certainly it does not.

Here are some more groups of three sentences, all of which are unsatisfactory in one way or another. Drawing on your knowledge, write a correct version of each.

1. (*a*) Either the Martians were clicking their space guns or checking their flamethrowers.
   (*b*) The Martians were clicking either their space guns or checking their flamethrowers.
   (*c*) The Martians either were clicking their space guns or checking their flamethrowers.
2. (*a*) Jumping out of bed, there was a blast of cold air from the open window.
   (*b*) There was a blast of cold air from the open window when jumping out of bed.
   (*c*) Jumping out of bed, a blast of cold air from the open window met him.
3. (*a*) A dungeon is where prisoners are kept.
   (*b*) Where prisoners are kept is called a dungeon.
   (*c*) Where prisoners are kept is what a dungeon is.
4. (*a*) Several linemen have been playing on this team and who earn five-figure salaries.
   (*b*) There have been several linemen playing on this team and who earn five-figure salaries.
   (*c*) This team has been played on by several linemen who earn five-figure salaries.

CHAPTER SIX

The Horizons of Grammar: Variety

English is a rich and varied language with many ways to express ideas. In this chapter we will consider first variety in words, and then variety in sentences.

VARIETY IN WORDS

A Strange Casement of the Poetic Apothecary

Poets are always in search of the right word, the
adjective that is inevitable,
Because an ill-chosen adjective induces levity in
the reader, and no poet wishes to be levitable.
A poem filled with the right words is more enjoyable,
and therefore takes longer to read;
Hence the old Louisiana saying "The *mot juste,*[1]
the less speed."
When, for instance, Keats refers to "magic" casements
he is no poetaster who a mass of trite, meaningless
phrases spawns; 5
He did not slap down the first adjective that came
to mind because he had left his thesarus at
Fanny Brawne's.
Whosoever thinks so, his ignorance of both Keats
and casements is absurd;
If Keats speaks of a casement as "opening," then
"magic" is the only possible word.
In the matter of casements Keats was no dreamy
lotophagic;[2]
He knew that if a casement was either openable or
shuttable it was manifestly magic. 10
Keats could have written a lot more odes and died
with money in the bank
But for the long hours he wasted trying to twist
little widgets that were rusted stuck and yanking
handles that wouldn't yank.
If his casements were like mine, when open they
would not admit the breeze, and when shut they
would not exclude the rain,
And when he looked through them he could not see
Shelley or anything else plain.

---

1 *Mot juste* (mō zhüst'): the most appropriate word.

2 *Lotophagic:* a person who eats lotus, a legendary fruit supposed to cause a dreamy happiness and forgetfulness.

So anybody who thinks there is a *juster mot* than
"magic," I suggest they join the lowing herd and
wind slowly o'er the lea, 15
And leave casements to Keats and to me.

From *Everyone but Thee and Me*
by Ogden Nash.

Mark Twain said, "The difference between the right word and the almost right word is the difference between lightning and the lightning bug." Choosing the right word is a constant problem in writing. Usually our fault lies in choosing a word that is too general to communicate a specific picture to our reader. In so doing we fall far short of Joseph Conrad's idea of the writer's purpose:

> My task is, by the power of the written word, to make you hear, to make you feel—it is, above all, to make you see.

Notice how this paragraph from Hemingway's "Big Two-Hearted River" skillfully involves our senses of sight and smell.

> He started a fire with some chunks of pine he got with the ax from a stump. Over the fire he stuck a wire grill, pushing the four legs down into the ground with his boot. Nick put the frying pan on the grill over the flames. He was hungrier. The beans and spaghetti warmed. Nick stirred them and mixed them together. They began to bubble, making little bubbles that rose with difficulty to the surface. There was a good smell. Nick got out a bottle of tomato catchup and out four slices of bread. The little bubbles were coming faster now. Nick sat down beside the fire and lifted the frying pan off. He poured about half the contents out into the tin plate. It spread slowly on the plate. Nick knew it was too hot. He poured on some tomato catchup. He knew the beans and spaghetti were still too hot. He looked at the fire, then at the tent, he was not going to spoil it all by burning his tongue. For years he had never enjoyed fried bananas because he had never been able to wait for them to cool. His tongue was very sensitive. He was very hungry. Across the river in the swamp, in the almost dark, he saw a mist rising. He looked at the tent once more. All right. He took a full spoonful from the plate.

From *The Hemingway Reader.*

The vividness is partially caused by Hemingway's variety in word choice. However, he deliberately repeats his set of key words. He uses controlled variety, not searching for strange synonyms. Skillful writing is the search for exact words and then the manipulation of them into a variety of contexts. For example, "They began to bubble, making little bubbles . . ." shows *bubble* as a verb and then a noun, in each case making us hear as well as see.

Exercise one. Here are two versions of "In Waste Places" by James Stephens. The second version is a revision of the first. Compare the two versions, observing how Stephens has changed his words. Explain several ways in which the words of the second version are more varied and unexpected than those of the first. (Incidentally, notice that in the fourth stanza of the second version Stephens has cut the longer sentences of the first version into shorter ones to convey his effect.)

The Waste Places

As a naked man I go
  Through the desert sore afraid,
Holding up my head although
  I'm as frightened as a maid.

The crouching lion there I saw   5
  From barren rocks lift up his eye;
He parts the cactus with his paw,
  And stares at me as I go by.

He would follow on my trace
  If he knew I was afraid, 10
If he knew my hardy face
  Hides the terrors of a maid.

In the night he rises and
  He stretches forth, he snuffs the air;
He roars and leaps along the sand, 15
  He creeps and watches everywhere.

His burning eyes, his eyes of bale,
  Through the darkness I can see;
He lashes fiercely with his tail,
  He would love to spring at me. 20

I am the lion in his lair;
  I am the fear that frightens me;
I am the desert of despair
  And the nights of agony.

Night or day, what'er befall, 25
  I must walk that desert land,
Until I can dare to call
  The lion out to lick my hand.

In Waste Places

As a naked man I go
Through the desert, sore afraid;
Holding high my head, although
I'm as frightened as a maid.

The lion crouches there! I saw 5
In barren rocks his amber eye!
He parts the cactus with his paw!
He stares at me, as I go by!

He would pad upon my trace
If he thought I was afraid! 10
If he knew my hardy face
Veils the terrors of a maid.

He rises in the night-time, and
He stretches forth! He snuffs the air!
He roars! He leaps along the sand! 15
He creeps! He watches everywhere!

His burning eyes, his eyes of bale
Through the darkness I can see!
He lashes fiercely with his tail!
He makes again to spring at me! 20

I am the lion, and his lair!
I am the fear that frightens me!
I am the desert of despair!
And the night of agony!

Night or day, whate'er befall, 25
I must walk that desert land,
Until I dare my fear, and call
The lion out to lick my hand!

Exercise two. Here is a list of adjectives that cluster around the idea of happiness. Although they have this similarity of lexical meaning, they do not all fit smoothly and appropriately into identical contexts. For instance, we say "Merry Christmas" but "Happy New Year"; we sometimes say "Happy Christmas" but hardly ever "Merry New Year." Invent contexts in which each will be the "right" word, creating as few contexts as possible to cover the entire list. In other words, you can fit several others into the Christmas and New Year patterns.

cheery	merry
mirthful	happy
gleeful	jolly
hilarious	joyful
glad	delightful

Exercise three. Suppose that you wrote this sentence in a story:

Three-year-old Michele went quickly down the street.

Your teacher suggests that you consult your thesaurus to find one word to replace the phrase *went quickly*. You do so and find these words:

speed, hie, hasten, spurt, sprint, scamper, scuttle, trip, post, scud, scurry, whiz, run, dart, swoop, fly, race, shoot, tear, whisk, sweep, skim, rush, dash, bolt, hurry, hasten, haste, accelerate, quicken.

Which words would definitely be unsuitable in the sentence about little Michele? Of the remaining words, which would you choose as the most appropriate? Why? Why may a thesaurus be a dangerous tool for the unwary writer?

Exercise four. Between 1922 and 1924 in Paris, Ernest Hemingway learned much about writing from Gertrude Stein, an older and established writer. Miss Stein emphasized the importance of repetition. Here is a paragraph from Hemingway's "Up in Michigan" which demonstrates how Hemingway applied her idea. *Like* appears as a verb in every sentence except the last. In the middle of the paragraph *like* appears as a preposition and in the last sentence as a gerund. Note also how flexibly and strangely Hemingway used *it* in six sentences in the paragraph.[3]

> Liz liked Jim very much. She liked it the way he walked over from the shop and often went to the kitchen door to watch for him to start down the road. She liked it about his mustache. She liked it about how white his teeth were when he smiled. She liked it very much that he didn't look like a blacksmith. She liked it how much D. J. Smith and Mrs. Smith liked Jim. One day she found that she liked it the way the hair was black on his arms and how white they were above the tanned line when he washed up in the washbasin outside the house. Liking that made her feel funny.

Write a paragraph repeating one of these words in a variety of transforms. Each word can occur as several parts of speech.

round   fast   up   down

Exercise five. Study this draft of "The Tyger" by William Blake, observing the several word-choices he considered as he was working on the poem. Then read his final version, in which his final choices appear. How and where does he achieve variety? What differences in spelling and punctuation do you observe in the two versions of the poem?

The Tyger

1 Tyger Tyger burning bright
In the forests of the night
What immortal hand & eye
or
Could frame thy fearful symmetry
Dare

[3] The quotation and ideas discussed here are drawn from Charles Fenton's *The Apprenticeship of Ernest Hemingway* (New American Library), pp. 123-124.

2 In what distant deeps or skies 5
Burnt in
Burnt the fire of thine eyes
The cruel
On what wings dare he aspire
What the hand dare seize the fire

3 And what shoulder & what art
Could twist the sinews of thy heart 10
And when thy heart began to beat
What dread hand & what dread feet

Could fetch it from the furnace deep
And in thy horrid ribs dare steep
In the well of sanguine woe 15
In what clay & in what mould
Were thy eyes of fury rolld

4 What the hammer what the chain
Where where
In what furnace was thy brain
What the anvil What the arm 20
grasp
clasp
dread grasp
Could its deadly terrors clasp
Dare grasp
clasp

6 Tyger Tyger burning bright
In the forests of the night
What immortal hand & eye
Dare form thy fearful symmetry 25
frame

2 Burnt in distant deeps or skies
The cruel fire of thine eyes
Could heart descend or wings aspire
What the hand dare seize the fire

5 And did he laugh his work to see 30
dare he smile
laugh
What the shoulder what the knee
ankle
Did he who made the lamb make thee
Dare
When the stars threw down their spears
And waterd heaven with their tears

Final Version

The Tiger

1 Tiger! Tiger! burning bright
In the forests of the night,
What immortal hand or eye
Could frame thy fearful symmetry?

2 In what distant deeps or skies 5
Burnt the fire of thine eyes?
On what wings dare he aspire?
What the hand dare seize the fire?

3 And what shoulder, and what art,
Could twist the sinews of thy heart? 10
And when thy heart began to beat,
What dread hand forged thy dread feet?

4 What the hammer? what the chain?
In what furnace was thy brain?
What the anvil? what dread grasp 15
Dare its deadly terrors clasp?

5 When the stars threw down their spears
And watered heaven with their tears,
Did he smile his work to see?
Did he who made the Lamb make thee? 20

6 Tiger! Tiger! burning bright
In the forests of the night,
What immortal hand or eye
Dare frame thy fearful symmetry?

VARIETY IN SENTENCES

In 1946, John Erskine said:

> When you write, you make a point, not by subtracting as though you sharpened a pencil, but by adding. When you put one word after another, your statement should be more precise the more you add. If the result is otherwise, you have added the wrong thing, or you have added more than was needed.[4]

Interested by Erskine's idea, Professor Francis Christensen of the University of Southern California tested it by collecting and analyzing thousands of sentences written by professional writers. From this research he gained many insights into their composition habits. Moreover, his insights show how we may use many of the grammatical ideas in this book to write sentences of greater vigor and variety. Of course there are many other ways to study composition, but Christensen's ideas are practical, fruitful, and exciting, especially for students of modern English grammar.

In modern prose, what does the successful writer start with and what does he add? He starts with a central sentence, standing as a unit in his longer sentence. A central sentence may be either basic or derived. Moreover, it is a special kind of receiver —one that accepts inserts at either end, but not in its middle. Around the central sentence the writer inserts transforms.

At the Beginning

At the beginning of the sentence the favorite inserts are adverbialization transforms or other adverbial elements: single-word adverbs and adverbial phrases with or without prepositions.

Single-word adverb:

Yesterday he slugged the commander.

Adverbial phrases:

Yesterday morning he slugged the commander.
At nine yesterday morning, he slugged the commander.

---

[4] In "A Note on the Writer's Craft," *Twentieth Century English,* quoted by Francis Christensen in "Notes toward a New Rhetoric," *College English* (October 1963), p. 12. This section has been influenced by Professor Christensen's ideas in this article as well as in "A Generative Rhetoric of the Sentence," *College Composition and Communication* (October 1963), pp. 1-7, and "In Defense of the Absolute," *College English* (April 1950), pp. 401-403.

Adverbialization transform:

When the clock struck nine yesterday morning, he slugged the commander.

Here are several adverbial openers from professional writers. The first group is from Katherine Anne Porter's "The Leaning Tower."

Single-word adverb:

Instantly, he regretted it, but there was no place to hide them from her.

Adverbial phrase:

Quite suddenly she gave a last plunge at a chair, set it in place with a thump, and ran away, her body full of awkward, contradictory motions.
At the foot of the shallow flight of steps leading to the new cabaret, a dish of food scraps had been set out for the hungry small animals.

Adverbialization transform:

When Rosa brought the coffee tray, one end of it was occupied by an ordinary looking black japanned metal box.

The second group is from Eudora Welty's "Powerhouse."

Single-word adverb:

Inside, sheltered dry smells stand like screens around a table covered with a red-checkered cloth, in the center of which flies hang onto an obelisk-shaped ketchup bottle.

Adverbial phrase:

Late at night they play the one waltz they will ever consent to play—by request, "Pagan Love Song."
After a long time, he holds up the number of fingers to tell the band how many choruses still to go—usually five.

Adverbialization transform:

When Powerhouse first came back from intermission, no doubt full of beer, they said, he got the band tuned up again in his own way.

In these examples, most of the adverbial sentence openers add the time of the central sentence. Only two add the place: *At the foot of the shallow flight of steps leading to the new cabaret* and *Inside.* Adverbial sentence openers can add other kinds of details too. For example, in this sentence from "The Wind and the Snow of Winter," Walter Van Tilburg Clark combines manner and place adverbials:

> *Slowly, with the blown snow behind them,* they came to the first built-up block and passed the first dim light showing through a smudged window under the arcade.

In this sentence from "The Cocoon," John B. L. Goodwin uses an adverbialization transform expressing the condition on which Denny's vowing depends:

> *If he survived the night* Denny vowed he would destroy the thing upon the wall . . .

In "A Country Love Story," Jean Stafford begins this sentence with an adverbialization transform expressing the cause of the postponement of the major repairs:

> *Because they had not moved in until July and by that time the workmen of the region were already engaged,* most of the major repairs of the house were to be postponed until the spring . . .

Single-word adverbs expressing concession very often open sentences of professional writers: *however, nevertheless, still.* Adverbial phrases of concession also appear, beginning with such words as *in spite of.* Here is an adverbialization transform of concession from H. L. Davis's "Open Winter":

> *Even though March had come,* it still blew, drying the ground deep, shrinking the water courses, beating back the clouds, . . .

Adverbial sentence openers can express other adverbial details too, but these we have mentioned are the most common.

Exercise one. Here is a set of sentences from *Henderson the Rain King* by Saul Bellow. Find each adverbial sentence opener, identify it as a single-word adverb, an adverbial phrase, or an adverbialization transform, and state what kind of detail it adds to its sentence.

1. Near me I then heard the snarl of a dog and I became more dangerous to him than he could possibly be to me.
2. As if he understood my terms, the examiner nodded, and I stripped off my T-shirt, which was greatly in need of a wash.
3. While I was still kidding like this the examiner continued to size me up.
4. From a scaffold at some distance to the left of the palace I saw, or thought I saw, bodies hanging upside down.
5. Under the thickened rain clouds, a heated, darkened breeze sprang up.
6. And then, after a great, neighing, cold blast of wind, the clouds opened and the rain began to fall.
7. Despite all the shocks of yesterday I was beginning to comprehend why I felt reassured at first sight of the king.
8. From top to bottom this fellow was clad in his dirty white, like kid leather, his hair covered with the chalky paste.
9. Thus it was entirely up to the king to complete the capture.
10. At the hips and feet the body was tied with thongs.
11. Fiercely, the old man started to yell at me.
12. So before pigs ever came on my horizon, I received a deep impression from a bear.

Exercise two. Here are three central sentences:

(*a*) Judge Thomas bandaged the wound swiftly.
(*b*) The canyon yawned in the moonlight.
(*c*) Teresa's raincoat will brush the scaffold.

To each sentence add adverbial openers as follows:

To the *a* sentence:

1. A single-word adverb expressing time.
2. An adverbial phrase expressing place.

To the *b* sentence:

1. An adverbial phrase expressing manner.
2. An adverbialization transform expressing cause.

To the *c* sentence:

1. A single-word adverb expressing concession.
2. An adverbialization transform expressing condition.

At the End

After his central sentence, the professional writer uses a variety of inserts produced by adjectivalization and adverbialization transformation. These inserts add layers of concrete details to his central sentence. Generally, the inserts are separated from the central sentence by commas, indicating that grammatically they are loosely connected to it. That is, the relative clauses and reduced relative clauses are appositive, not restrictive; the adverbialization transforms are movable, not essential parts of the predicate in the central sentence. These facts are summarized in the following table.

Inserts Produced by Adjectivalization

Relative Clause

The little girl took off her shoes, *which were soaked with rain.*

From: The little girl took off her shoes. (Receiver)
Her shoes were soaked with rain. (Insert)

Reduced Relative Clauses

Verb Phrase:

The little girl took off her shoes, *soaked with rain.*

From the same two sentences, with only the verb phrase of the insert retained.

Noun Phrase:

The little girl took off her shoes, *blobs of soggy leather.*

From: The little girl took off her shoes. (Receiver)
Her shoes were blobs of soggy leather. (Insert)

Only the predicate noun phrase of the insert is retained.

Adjective Phrase:

The little girl took off her shoes, *soggy with rain.*

From: The little girl took off her shoes. (Receiver)
Her shoes were soggy with rain. (Insert)

Only the adjective phrase of the insert is retained.

Single-Word Adjectives:

The little girl took off her shoes, *soggy, dirty, old.*

From: The little girl took off her shoes. (Receiver)
Her shoes were soggy. (Insert)
Her shoes were dirty. (Insert)
Her shoes were old. (Insert)

Only the adjectives of the inserts are retained.

Inserts Produced by Adverbialization

Adverbialization Transform

Bernice was giggling madly, *although her eyes were flooding with tears.*

Absolute:

Bernice was giggling madly, *her eyes flooding with tears.*

Here the full adverbialization transform has been reduced by the omissions of the subordinator *although* and the *be* auxiliary.

Absolute:

Bernice was giggling madly, *her eyes full of tears.*

From: Bernice was giggling madly. (Receiver)
Her eyes were full of tears. (Insert)

Here the subordinator and the *be* main verb have been omitted.

Here is an assortment of final-position inserts from "Winter Dreams" by F. Scott Fitzgerald.

Relative Clause

Miss Jones and her retinue now withdrew, and at a proper distance from Dexter became involved in a heated conversation, *which was concluded by Miss Jones taking one of the clubs and hitting it on the ground with violence.*

Reduced Relative Clauses

Noun Phrases:

This was his girl who was speaking, *his own, his beautiful, his pride.*

Judy Jones had left a man and crossed the room to him—*Judy Jones, a slender enamelled doll in cloth of gold: gold in a band at her head, gold in two slipper points at her dress's hem.*

Verb Phrases:

She called everyone darling, *endowing the endearment with careless, individual camaraderie.*

A low, pale oblong detached itself suddenly from the darkness of the Island, *spitting forth the reverberate sound of a racing motor-boat.*

It was a curious day, *slashed abruptly with fleeting, familiar impressions.*

Adjective Phrase:

The little girl who had done this was eleven—*beautifully ugly as little girls are apt to be who are destined after a few years to be inexpressibly lovely and bring no end of misery to a great number of men.*

Single-word Adjectives:

The dark street lightened, the dwellings of the rich loomed up around them, he stopped his coupé in front of the great white bulk of the Mortimer Joneses' house, *somnolent, gorgeous,* drenched with the splendor of the damp moonlight.

Adverbialization Transform

She would forgive him, *because it was not a matter of any moment but rather something to be brushed aside lightly.*

Absolutes:

When he looked around again the girl was standing up on the rushing board, *her arms spread wide, her eyes lifted toward the moon.*

Exercise one. Identify the absolutes in the following sentences.

1. . . . Wilson swayed, his right arm hanging useless, blood beginning to show in a small stream from under the sleeve over the hand, the gun slipping from the numbing fingers. (From *Shane* by Jack Schaefer.)

2. While they were read, he lay back against the wall, his eyes closed, his thin, horny hand pulling at his light beard, and listened to the voices and the orchestras and the single instruments in his mind. (From "The Portable Phonograph" by Walter Van Tilburg Clark.)
3. For the first time she was really sure he would be waiting for her, and she hurried up the three blocks, the skirt of the print dress swinging under her coat, and turned into her own block. (From "The Demon Lover" by Shirley Jackson.)
4. The door swung open beneath her hand and she saw the empty attic room, bare lath on the walls, floorboards unpainted. (From "The Demon Lover" by Shirley Jackson.)
5. During the day it was a thunderous surge of cars, the gas stations open, a great insect rustling and ceaseless jockeying for position as the scarab beetles, a faint incense puttering from their exhausts, skimmed homeward to the far horizons. (From "The Pedestrian" by Ray Bradbury.)
6. They stepped down into the areaway in front of the entrance, the car door banging hollowly behind them. (From "In Greenwich There Are Many Gravelled Walks" by Hortense Calisher.)

Exercise two. Using the central sentences below, transform their partner sentences according to the directions given, and insert each at the end of its central sentence. Example:

Central sentence: Cronley winked at his sister.
Absolute: Cronley's eyes flashed with fun.
Result: Cronley winked at his sister, his eyes flashing with fun.

1. *Central sentence:* The forward pass is high and wide.
   Verb phrase: The forward pass is spiraling into the wind.
2. *Central sentence:* Smirker trotted back to the dugout.
   Adverbialization transform: The coach smiled at Smirker.
3. *Central sentence:* Mr. Tanford's heart stood still.
   Adjective phrase: Mr. Tanford's heart was taut with disgust.
4. *Central sentence:* He stood in the tower trembling.
   Absolute: His clothes were sodden from the freezing rain.
5. *Central sentence:* The plane gave a gentle lurch.
   Noun phrase: The lurch was a warning of disaster.

6. *Central sentence:* A girl in a deck chair was teasing a beagle.
   Relative clause: The beagle yawned and tried to lick her hand.
7. *Central sentence:* Pa poured milk over his bowl of dry cereal.
   Verb phrase: Pa dug up the flap on the milk carton with his fingernail.
8. *Central sentence:* Her voice faltered.
   Adverbialization transform: She tried to hold back her tears.
9. *Central sentence:* Willis leafed through the phone book quickly.
   Adjective phrase: Willis was eager to hear her voice again.
10. *Central sentence:* Brock was not disturbed by her laughter.
    Absolute: Brock's face was yellow and unshaven.
11. *Central sentence:* He stepped back from his wife.
    Relative clause: His wife was teetering on the edge of the diving board.

Exercise three. Convert the insert at the end of each of these sentences into a full separate sentence. Identify the insert as absolute, noun phrase, verb phrase, adjective phrase, adverbialization transform, or relative clause.

1. He strode out of the bargain center, his arms loaded with awkward packages.
2. Isabel was sitting in the taxi, breathing the smoky air.
3. The hall was a long room, colored yellow.
4. Even her children knew her for what she was, shallow, heartless, vain.
5. He was living in hotels then, moving from one to another every five days.
6. He pounded the table with his club, a gnarled branch of oak.
7. The plane reached the eye of the hurricane, which was roaring in at a rate of a hundred miles an hour.

Sentence Outlines

We can outline the shape of sentences and thus show the relationships between the central sentence and its inserts. Here is the outline of a sentence from Elizabeth Parsons' "The Nightingales Sing."

In the darkness she heard the wind rising around Sandy's house, breathing over the open hill, whistling softly in the wet, rusted window screens, stirring in the apple trees.

Adverbial Phrase	In the darkness
Central Sentence	she heard the wind
Verb Phrase	rising around Sandy's house,
Verb Phrase	breathing over the open hill,
Verb Phrase	whistling softly in the wet, rusted window screens,
Verb Phrase	stirring in the apple trees.

The central sentence, *she heard the wind,* is written flush with the lefthand margin. However, the complete sentence actually opens with an adverbial phrase, *in the darkness.* This is written on the line above the central sentence because it stands first in the sentence, but it is indented to show that it is an insert. In other words, the order of the inserts is maintained in our outline of the sentence. The four verb phrases, *rising around Sandy's house, breathing over the open hill, whistling softly in the wet, rusted window screens,* and *stirring in the apple trees,* add details to the central sentence and therefore are indented equally. Thus the indentations graph the relationship among the parts of the total sentence.

Sentences written by professional writers can be much more complicated than this one. Look at this sentence of Willa Cather's from "A Death in the Desert," which is graphed to show the relationships among its parts.

He opened the letter, his lashes half-veiling his kind eyes, and saw to his satisfaction that it was a long one—wonderfully tactful and tender, even for Adriance, who was tender with his valet and his stable boy, with his old gondolier and the beggar women who prayed to the saints for him.

Central Sentence	He opened the letter,
Absolute	his lashes half-veiling his kind eyes,
Central Sentence	and saw to his satisfaction that it was a long one—
Adjective Phrase	wonderfully tactful and tender,
Adverbial Phrase	even for Adriance,
Relative Clause	who was tender with his valet and his stable boy, with his old gondolier and the beggar women who prayed to the saints for him.

This sentence has its central sentence split into two parts, the result of a conjunction transformation. The first half of the central sentence has an absolute inserted into it, while the second half of the central sentence has three inserts with insertions: a relative clause inserted into an adverbial phrase inserted into an adjective phrase. The graph shows all these relationships.

Exercise one. Starting with each of the short central sentences given below, add one insert after it, a different type in each case. Label the type you use in each sentence. Examples (from "The Easter Egg Party" by Elizabeth Bowen):

> *Central Sentence:* One by one children bounded off from the others,
> *Verb Phrase:* glancing jealously round to see that no one was on their tracks.
>
> *Central Sentence:* The big scandal only broke at the end of teatime,
> *Adverbialization Transform:* when Eunice began to check up the eggs found.
>
> *Central Sentence:* Hermione gave the green box a last look,
> *Noun Phrase:* the first fully human look she had spent on anything since she came to West Wallows.
>
> *Central Sentence:* She shook hands with a rigid arm
> *Relative Clause:* on which all the bracelets jumped.

Here are the central sentences you are to use:

1. The sun shines continuously.
2. The doctor lit the match.
3. The search party turned away sadly.

Exercise two. Write three sentences with two or three parallel inserts following the central sentence. That is, use two adverbialization transforms, two adjective phrases, two absolutes, and so on. Invent your own central sentences. Examples (from William Faulkner's *The Old Man):*

Central Sentence: . . . they passed another huddle of mules,
Absolute: the eyeballs rolling too,
Absolute: the long morose faces turning into and out of the firelight . . .

Central Sentence: It was raining steadily now
Adverbial Phrase: though still not hard,
Adverbial Phrase: still without passion . . .

Central Sentence: He carried nothing else,
Noun Phrase: no food,
Noun Phrase: no change of clothes,
Noun Phrase: not even a coat.

Central Sentence: He caught the woman beneath the arms,
Verb Phrase: dragging her out of the boat,
Verb Phrase: plunging and panting after the vanished deer.

Exercise three. Write three sentences, each with one adverbial opener and one insert following the central sentence. Vary them interestingly and freely. Name the types of openers and inserts you use. Here are two examples from professional writers.

Then she locked the doors front and back. *(Frank O'Connor)*
Adverb Central Sentence. Adverbial phrase

When the day began to cool and shorten,
Adverbialization Transform
a cricket came to bless their house
Central Sentence
nightly singing behind the kitchen stove.
Verb Phrase *(Jean Stafford)*

Exercise four. This sentence is from James Baldwin's *Go Tell It on the Mountain.*

Adverb	Nevertheless,
Adverbialization Transform	when she came to die,
Relative Clause	which she did eventually,
Verb Phrase	looking more grotesque than ever,
Adverbialization Transform	as she deserved,
Central Sentence	his thoughts were abruptly arrested, and he was chilled by the expression on her face.

In this sentence we find dense layers of details. An adverbialization transform and a verb phrase are inserted within a relative clause inserted into another adverbialization transform. This whole structure, along with another adverb, is inserted into the central sentence, which appears at the end of the sequence. It itself is produced by a conjunction transformation. James Baldwin writes richly complex sentences.

Analyze these sentences by indentation and outline, and identify their inserts as adverbs, adverbial phrases, adverbialization transforms, relative clauses, noun phrases, verb phrases, adjectives, adjective phrases, or absolutes.

1. When they lifted her from the lighter, the water would stream from her sides, back into the sea. *(Daphne DuMaurier)*
2. The next day he looked down on the city from the air, burnished in sunlight, toylike, precise. *(Carson McCullers)*
3. As they went toward the house, it loomed up above them, twice its size, the kitchen windows throwing low beams of light out into the fog. *(Elizabeth Parsons)*
4. All through the night, first at the window, then at the door, the beating of wings continued, relieved only by the occasional plop of the soft, heavy body. *(John B. L. Goodwin)*
5. The guards herded the convicts into them, three brace of shackled men to each tent. *(William Faulkner)*
6. He lay flat on his face, slightly spread-eagled and in an attitude almost peaceful, a kind of abject meditation. *(William Faulkner)*
7. Then it began to rain again, as upon a signal, while they stood or squatted in their harsh garments which

had not dried out during the night but had merely become slightly warmer than the air. *(William Faulkner)*

8. With both hands free he now dragged himself over the stern and lay prone on his face, streaming with blood and water and panting, not with exhaustion but with that furious rage which is terror's aftermath. *(William Faulkner)*
9. He clung to it, not instinctively against the time when he would be back inside the boat and would need it, because for a time he did not believe he would ever regain the skiff or anything else that would support him, but because he did not have time to think about turning it loose. *(William Faulkner)*
10. So he rose, out of the watery scarlet puddle in which he had lain, streaming, the soaked denim heavy as iron on his limbs, the black hair plastered to his skull, the blood-infused water streaking his jumper, and dragged his forearm gingerly and hurriedly across his lower face and glanced at it then grasped the paddle and began to try to swing the skiff upstream. *(William Faulkner)*

Exercise five. Construct one derived sentence from each of the following outlines. For example:

Adverbialization
  Transform: After the day ended,
Central Sentence: they hurried home
Verb Phrase: bubbling with joy.

1. Central Sentence,
   Verb Phrase.
2. Central Sentence,
   Noun Phrase.
3. Adverbial Phase,
   Central Sentence,
   Relative Clause.
4. Adverbialization Transform,
   Central Sentence,
   Adjective Phrase,
   Adjective Phrase.
5. Adverbial Phrase,
   Central Sentence,
   Absolute,
   Absolute.
6. Central Sentence,
   Adverbialization Transform.

7. Adverb,
   Central Sentence,
   Noun Phrase,
   Noun Phrase.
8. Central Sentence,
   Noun Phrase,
   Absolute.

Exercise six. Now try these outlines, making more densely detailed sentences.

1. Central Sentence,
   Verb Phrase,
   Relative Clause,
   Verb Phrase,
   Absolute.
2. Central Sentence,
   Adjective Phrase,
   Relative Clause,
   Adverbialization Transform.
3. Adverbialization Transform,
   Central Sentence,
   Noun Phrase,
   Relative Clause,
   Adjective Phrase,
   Verb Phrase,
   Adverbialization Transform.

Exercise seven. Here is a set of sentences by professional writers. Analyze these sentences to identify the inserts in each. Then write your own sentence following the outline of each of these sentences.

1. From the other window, if the bed was turned, you could see the town, with a little smoke above it, and the Dawson mountains looking like real mountains with the snow on them. *(Ernest Hemingway)*
2. Suddenly, she was touching some heavy crimson roses that were soft as velvet, touching them thoughtfully, without knowing, as a mother sometimes fondles the hand of her child. *(D. H. Lawrence)*
3. In the circle of the lamplight the two men still bent over the table looking at the flies. *(Caroline Gordon)*
4. With her hand on her knees, the old woman waited, silent, erect and motionless, just as if she were in armour. *(Eudora Welty)*

5. We saddled up the mare and went across the lot, where limestone bunched out of the ground and cedar trees and blue grass grew out of the split rock. *(Robert Penn Warren)*
6. The policemen lingered a moment in the elevator, facing the Chandlers, who hung together in the doorway like the host couple after a shindig. *(John Updike)*

Exercise eight. Select one of your sentences from *Exercise seven* and graph it on a sentence outline. Then expand each level of your outline to a full sentence.

Index